Mongolian Love Letters

Also by the Author

Serenade of the Sasquatch
Music of the Mermaids

Mongolian Love Letters

Finding My Footing at the Edge of the World

Rachael Lundin

Published by Horizon Line Books Wenatchee, Washington
ISBN: 979-8-9946979-0-0

Author's Note: This book is a work of memoir. It reflects the author's recollections of experiences over time. Some names and identifying characteristics have been changed, some events have been compressed, and some dialogue has been recreated from memory.

Library of Congress Control Number: 2026907375
First Edition

Printed in the United States of America

For Breezy, who carried a lonely
twelve-year-old girl into a world of possibility.

For Roan, who felt every storm and waited anyway.

For My Little Pony, who said "Hi! Did you know
we're on an adventure?" at exactly the right moment.

Good horses, all.

Contents

Foreword

September 20, 2022

It is a rare privilege to witness someone confront the very hardest thing they can imagine in order to heal from indescribable loss, and to do so with unwavering dedication to a vision larger than themselves. Rachael Lundin is one of those rare people. This book, born in a time when the world seemed to have gone mad, is the product of her remarkable resilience, stalwart endurance, relentless commitment to excellence, and profound love.

I had the honor of riding alongside her on the Gobi Gallop which, at 700 kilometers in just 10 days of riding, is the longest annual charity horseback ride on the planet and a feat requiring tremendous physical, emotional, and psychological endurance. Originally planned for 2020, Rachael's Gobi Gallop had been postponed due to COVID, which meant we rode in September instead of June when the Gobi Gallop usually runs. The days were short and every moment of daylight was precious. Along the way, nature threw its challenges at us—searing heat, unending wind, and even waking to four or five inches of snow. Each day's ride required careful attention to preserve the horses' strength while still moving forward, which meant endless hours of trotting, incredibly sore muscles, and fatigue like nothing you can imagine.

Her smile and laughter lit the hardest days, and through them, she led all of us to give our best, to honor the journey, embrace the vision, and care deeply for the children who are the soul of this project. This book is more than a collection of words and experiences; it is a testament to Rachael's courage, her ability to persevere through grief and tragedy, and her unwavering belief in the power of determination and compassion. I am not only proud of her achievements but profoundly inspired by the strength she shows in carrying on, always moving forward, always seeking to make a difference.

May this book remind you, as it has reminded me, that even in the hardest moments, vision, determination, and love can carry us through—and that the work of the heart is always worth it.

Julie Veloo
Veloo Foundation, Vice President
Gobi Gallop Expedition Chief

1

Where Do I Start?

Dear Charlie,

How do I even begin to tell this story? Some letters are written in ink, others in miles traveled and mountains crossed. This one begins with the rumble of horses hooves.

The Mongolian Steppe had no mercy after sunset. The night consumed everything. The cloud cover meant no stars, no moon—just utter black with no way to differentiate ground from sky.

Darkness, however, did not mean silence.

The wind, ever-present, whooshed and moaned, cut only by the whinnies of our horses. I have learned that horses have different kinds of whinnies: soft nickers for greetings and loud bellows to welcome a friend at a distance. My horse's sounds were becoming something else altogether. His high-pitched panicked whinnies called desperately for his herd. With each cry, his muscles tensed beneath me, coiling like a spring. He was going to bolt any moment. I could not let that happen.

Somewhere ahead, our team had disappeared. Beside me, Brandon's voice echoed my fears. "I can't see them anymore, can you?"

"No."

I gripped my reins tighter and tried to project confidence I didn't feel. Two years of planning, one devastating loss, and ten days of riding had led to this moment: lost on the other side of the world, trying to convince a nervous horse that I knew what I was doing.

I didn't.

I couldn't see my horse, let alone the ground beneath us. The flat terrain had vanished, replaced by a series of rises and falls that rolled beneath our horses like waves in a storm. Each downward plunge made my stomach lurch, my tired muscles screaming while I tried to maintain balance. The leather reins, slick with sweat—mine or the horse's, I couldn't tell—threatened to slip through my cramping fingers.

"It's OK, you got this," I said, my voice spilling out whatever soothing sounds came to mind. The words were nonsense, but I desperately needed my horse to believe them, and to believe he was better off with me than running full tilt into nothingness.

"But we must be going the right way. They have to be out there somewhere," Brandon said—more to himself than to me, I thought.

He was right; they were out there, somewhere. Everything was out there, somewhere. Home was somewhere. Safety was somewhere. Our team was somewhere. But we were nowhere, navigating by faith and our horses' instincts through the moonless night.

I thought of you then, as I had so many times during this journey. What would you say if you could see me now? Your worry for me in that moment would have been palpable. I was trusting my life to a horse I barely knew, in a night so complete it felt solid.

A tree materialized, a denser shadow against the void. My horse swerved. I caught my breath and forced out words of encouragement: "You got this. It's going to be OK."

I wasn't convincing anyone.

2

Preparation and Departure

The Beginning

If I had gone to Mongolia when I first read about it, I would have had a very different experience. I was stable then—strong, confident, and eager to test myself. I hadn't yet learned how little of what I thought of as my strength was actually Charlie's. And how quickly it could be snatched away.

We were in our living room when I got the text from a friend that said, "This made me think of you."

I always wanted a living room cluttered with things from my travels. Knickknacks and strange objects from around the globe. An actual globe, big and centered, and pictures on the wall of us in exotic locations. I wanted proof that we had lived. That I had stories to tell.

But we didn't have the money for such things. I grew up one of two daughters of a single mother who did her best with what she had. An over-read, lonely child, with an imagination to turn everything into a potential adventure, I made do. And so now, instead of travel souvenirs, our living room was filled with paper maps of the world that I asked Charlie to frame in white trim and colorful paintings of exotic places—paint by numbers, if you must know—cobbled streets framed by outdoor restaurants and girls selling flowers, and azure Mediterranean coastlines inviting you to go sailing.

The room had a large bookcase that Charlie built for me, a fireplace that he tended faithfully, and a large cream-colored sectional sofa.

The sectional was my dream sofa. Some people have dream cars or dream houses. I had a dream sofa. Raising our girls in a tiny cabin in the woods, where wind whispered through pine needles and coyotes sang us to sleep, we never had enough seating for all of us to be in the same room at the same time without being very cuddly.

The cabin was barely 900 square feet of creaking floorboards and stubbed toes, where you couldn't open the fridge if someone was standing at the sink. Not a bad thing, really, but when three girls turned into three teens who were "so over it," with backpacks and sports gear exploding from every corner, space became a big deal. I desperately wanted a couch we could all be on in the rare moments it was OK to hug them.

The sofa came after all that, when only one teen was still home, the others having flown the nest and dealing with their own small-space challenges. Still, I loved that sofa for its potential.

In the meantime, Charlie and I sat on it, side by side, as if the rest of the sofa did not exist, our legs and arms touching while we independently scrolled through our phones. The fabric was warm where we touched, cool everywhere else. The fire popped and hissed in the background, filling the room with the sweet-sharp scent of wood smoke. He wore his usual evening uniform—a worn t-shirt over a gray long john top, carpenter jeans soft from a hundred washes. The winter night pressed against our windows, making our bubble of warmth feel even more precious.

Charlie and I were makers. We had that much in common. Charlie liked woodworking—his hands carried the evidence of fine sawdust caught in his nail beds and the occasional nick or splinter he'd removed with his pocketknife. The garage was his sanctuary, where the sweet smell of fresh-cut pine mixed with machine oil and neat stacks of lumber awaited his next project. Each piece of wood was a conversation to Charlie; he'd run his palm over the grain like someone reading braille, listening with his fingers until the wood revealed its secrets. Standing a few inches taller than my five-foot-six frame, he often reached things down for me, his blue eyes smiling.

I preferred painting, crafting, and welding. My workspace was a curated explosion of creativity—half-finished canvases, the sharp ozone smell of hot metal, and bins overflowing with possibilities: bits of copper wire, sea glass, scraps of interesting paper, and old bicycle gears. I'd lose track of time in there, emerging hours later covered in paint splatters or metal shavings, my steel-gray hair escaping its tie in flyaway wisps. Once I even set my hair on fire with a stray ember, which Charlie never let me forget. "My personal centerfold," he teased, watching me storm out of my workshop, flushed and muscled from gym sessions, my sharp edges softened by an extra five pounds that refused to budge. We both hunted for connections between disparate things, finding beauty in joining unlike pieces together.

Other than that, our interests didn't match up.

Charlie liked old westerns and war movies. I liked fantasy and sci-fi. He enjoyed watching lawn mower reviews on YouTube. I enjoyed watching mounted archery. But we liked each other, despite that.

So, when I said, "Oh Charlie, listen to this," my voice lifting in excitement, he put down his phone and listened. My heart was already racing, the words on my screen blurring as I leaned forward, trying to read faster, to consume it all at once.

The Gobi Gallop: Longest Annual Charity Ride on the Planet! This ride is only for the truly intrepid adventurer. 700 kilometers, or 450 miles, over ten riding days across country that created and formed the Mongolian hordes and Genghis Khan. A hard land, made beautiful by its sheer vastness. Pick a starting point and ride in any direction, not just an hour, or a day, but for days upon days upon days, and never meet a fence. But you will meet imposing mountains, plunging canyons, vast open plains, wild rivers, wilderness, extreme heat, extreme cold, rocks, dust, wind, and gopher holes. Traveling through this space at the speed of a horse brings it all close and real in a way that you can only experience to know.

The horses in question are ancestors of the steeds who carried Genghis Khan's Horde. To say they are tough is like saying Mount Rainier is tall. Powerful legs beating a steady rhythm in time to the music of the wind, they are bred for endurance and efficiency, and this land, with all its challenges and dangers, is their home. Their horsey minds have adapted to this space by an increased herd mentality. Sticking together is survival. As a group, they fend off wolves and starvation, and only by group consent do they allow themselves to be caught up and ridden by the two-legged creatures who think they own them.

The ride began in 2013 as the brainchild of Julie Veloo as a fundraiser to help children living in poverty in Ulaanbaatar. Refugees of climate change, which is stealing graze land and turning it into desert at the rate of 1,300 square miles per year, families who have made their living in the nomadic lifestyle flood the city in the hope of new opportunities. You know how it goes: The city bulges at the seams, not able to contain, let alone accommodate, all the needs of all its people, and still they come.

But there is magic here too. If you can dream it, you can do it, and Julie's dream was a school. This school would be in the highest poverty-stricken, least-served neighborhood—the garbage dump. It would be a safe place for children while their parents did what they needed to do to survive. It would provide healthy meals, clean clothes, singing, learning, growing, and the nurturing of the rising generation. And through the magic that is Mongolia, buildings have been donated, land obtained, teachers hired, and all the things needed to support 150 children from ages two years old through pre-K came together because of the fundraising efforts of the Gobi Gallop.

It was the phrase, "ride 700K and never meet a fence" that hooked me. I fantasized about days that started with sunrise yoga and ended with campfire-lit faces that told stories and sang songs. I pictured laughter and pleasant exhaustion and never-ending views.

"Ride the Gobi Gallop?" they asked.

"I want to do this," I said.

And Charlie said, "How can I help?"

What a gift it is to have a partner.

What loss when he is taken.

Naked Man Alert

Charlie and I went for a walk down at Riverfront Park. It was early morning, before the heat set in. We had just finished cleaning the horse stalls at the stables, where we boarded my horse, Roan. Charlie had a headache, but he still wanted to hang out with me.

Cleaning stalls is about 10 percent saying "hi" to the horses, breathing in their scent, and being in the moment. The other 90 percent is a hodgepodge of existential crisis, deep thoughts, or coming up with the next hare-brained idea. I had an idea that morning, something about putting together painting kits for people visiting the area. They could pick up their kit and take it to the park and paint for the day. Maybe a picnic lunch could be included. So, on the way home from the stables, we swung by the park to scope it out.

The rolling grass hills, the creek with the bridge, the old barn, and the trail that led to the river—all of it perfect inspiration for any wannabe artist. Charlie listened as I planned it all out.

While I talked, we wandered to the dock below the barn, which was hidden from view unless you were right on it. We stood there, listening to the park wake up. Birdsong permeated the morning mist, mixing with the gentle lap of water against the dock and the rhythmic dip of a distant paddle. I looked toward the sound as a paddle boarder came around the corner. His board cut through the rising mist.

"Is that man naked?" I asked Charlie. He looked and then looked away fast.

"Yep," he said.

We both turned our backs and laughed our way back to the car.

Charlie spent the rest of the day trying to get on top of his headache. I spent mine happily scheming. I met a friend for coffee that afternoon. I told her about the naked man.

When I got home, Charlie was in the dark bedroom, moaning. I went to check on him. I massaged his neck and told him about the coffee. We chuckled again about the naked man.

Charlie lived with chronic pain, the result of a terrible accident involving a building that collapsed on him and trapped him for thirty-six hours. It happened in February, in the heart of the Cascade Mountains, so there was snow and freezing temperatures. His body was crushed, like an aluminum pop can.

It was his dog who led rescuers to his location. She had been trying to dig him out, her paws bloody with the effort. He was flown to Harborview, where he spent more than four months recovering. He was told he would never walk again.

He did walk again, but only after years of rehabilitation. When he graduated from wheelchair to walker, he began building his log cabin. When he graduated from walker to cane, he walked to the end of the driveway and sat down, where he waited until his dad pulled in from work. And together they walked back home. Charlie never graduated high school, but he graduated from every challenge life threw at him through sheer determination and grit.

My Charlie was a survivor. And for many years, he saw continuous improvement. But in the last few years, he'd started losing ground. He slept a lot. He had headaches. Chronic pain was the third person in our marriage.

But this headache was different somehow. I couldn't tell you how. Maybe it was the way his face looked more gray than usual, or how his usual jokes about his pain were absent, replaced by a silence that seemed to fill our bedroom. Whatever it was, something in my gut twisted when I looked at him. I had already changed into pajamas and helped Charlie do the same when I made a decision. "Let's go to the ER, Charlie."

And he said, "I don't know what they can do for me."

"I don't know either, but people go with migraines all the time. They give them a shot, and it helps."

"OK," Charlie said.

This was Tuesday, August 17, 2021. I was not allowed back with him, due to Covid. I hugged him and said, "I love you. I'll be right here when you are done."

I spent my time scrolling through Realtor sites, dreaming about a house where we could have Roan on the property with us. At one point, they called a "code blue" over the intercom. I had recently learned that code blue was used when someone had stopped breathing. I said a prayer for the doctors, the patient, and the family and went back to scrolling. My daughter texted me, "Where are you guys?" I texted back that we were in the ER, but nothing to worry about. We would be home soon.

Finally, the doctor came out. He called my name and then invited me into a side room to talk. I thought he took me to the private room because he was concerned about patient confidentiality.

And then he told me the news. Charlie had had a seizure. They put him in a scanner and learned that he had a brain bleed. They needed to fly him to Harborview. Did I have any questions? Each statement sounded like a foreign language. I couldn't quite comprehend the words.

I don't really want to tell you about the rest. Even now, years later, my hands shake as I type these words and my throat tightens around memories I wish I could soften. But I made a promise to tell this story, so let me tell you about standing on the helicopter pad watching them load the love of my life. The whop whop whop of the helicopter blades as they sped up. How I tried to make myself as small as possible, hunched in, afraid that if I moved too fast, or caused any kind of inconvenience to anyone, that I would make the chaos worse. I don't want to tell you how the next morning, security at Harborview almost threw me out because they thought I was a homeless person who somehow had gotten past them. I don't want to tell you about the far corner of the cafeteria where I sat, calling my list of people. The coffee in front of me going cold, untouched. How between each call I sobbed, breathed, collected myself, found calm, and then dialed the next number. How my voice grew hoarse, but the words stayed the same, each time just as impossible to say as before. How the fluorescent lights made everything feel surreal, like I was watching someone else's tragedy unfold. How a kind stranger slipped a napkin onto my table and rushed away. The napkin said, "Thinking of you today...you're held in thought and loving energy."

I'm sure you have already guessed that Charlie did not survive this ordeal, though it would be twelve days before he passed away. A twelve-day journey from hope to devastation. If you have lived any time at all on this planet, then you know your world can change in a moment.

For me, it was twelve days of sitting in the ICU chair, watching the monitors' steady rhythm, trying to find words for my Facebook updates that would convey hope without promising too much. The nurses moved around us with practiced efficiency, their shoes squeaking on the linoleum floor. I kept thinking about our morning at the park, how just days ago we had laughed about the naked paddleboarder, how normal everything had been. How you never know when your last normal moment will be.

Final Facebook Update August 29, 2021

Charlie has been declared deceased. He was an organ donor, and soon some lucky recipient will carry his heart. I dreamt last night that he got out of bed and was walking away, and the nursing staff didn't notice. I was yelling at them that he needed his helmet on (they had removed a portion of his skull during surgery, after all), and he put his hand on my arm and said, "No, I don't, honey." His touch felt so real—warm and solid, the way he always steadied me when I was worrying too much. I believe he was saying goodbye to me then. There will be dark days ahead, but for now, I have a measure of peace. I will be carrying the echo of his touch and the sound of his voice saying "honey" one last time.

A Measure of Peace? Ha!

My final Facebook post told everyone that I had a "measure of peace," which I suppose was true for a few minutes. Maybe even for a few days. Peace in the way that shock is peaceful. A silence and a feeling of slow motion. Of looking and not seeing. Of hearing but not listening. Like those stories you hear of buildings exploding and people afterward wandering down the street completely naked and totally dazed. That was the kind of peace I was feeling. I talked. I drove places. I did things. I was calm. I was reasonable. And then, suddenly, I would start screaming.

Songs on the radio became scalpels, slicing me open. Songs I was familiar with and could sing along to. They eased their way into my brain like old friends and then destroyed me with lyrics that never before meant what they meant now. For example, when Lewis Capaldi's voice filled my car speakers, singing *Someone You Loved*. I turned the volume higher and higher and by the time he got to the end, I was screaming along with him, trying to make the music louder than the silence Charlie left behind.

Dammit, Charlie! You are not here! What the hell?

The Application Process

But I promised you a story about Mongolia, so let's get back to that, shall we?

If I had been able to go to Mongolia the day I completed my interview, even then, it would have been a different experience.

On that day, I was still a whole person, not just a surviving husk who would later pack her bags based on an outdated packing list she excavated from the bottom of a pile of bills.

"Tell me about your travel experience," Julie asked through my laptop screen. We were interviewing through a Zoom call, and on the line was Julie Veloo, the founder of the Gobi Gallop, and Ryan, who was her assistant.

They didn't let just anyone go on the Gobi Gallop. It was too long, too arduous, and too remote. Once the ride started, there would be no easy way back. The people on the ride at the start were the ones you were stuck with for the entire trip. They needed riders who could handle the challenges. So you had to apply, and that process included an interview.

I answered her question by telling them about our trip to Africa. How Charlie and I took a working vacation to help women living with HIV. I told them about the long flights and acclimating to the climate. About the work, the search for supplies, and about our efforts to build a goat-milking station to make the job easier on the backs of the women who already lived with constant pain. We had empathy for pain, Charlie and I.

Julie was in her *ger*, the traditional canvas and wooden lattice home of the Mongolian Steppe. Ryan was in his apartment in the United States. I was in my bedroom in Washington State. I could see the orange patterns of the ger walls behind Julie, delightful swirls and motifs that seemed to dance in the shifting light from her window. Behind Ryan I could see horse tack hanging on hooks, the leather worn and well-used, furry hats that made me think of steppes and adventures, and a guitar propped in the corner. Behind me was only a bold green wall, waiting to be filled with images from Mongolia. Charlie had questioned the color choice but painted it with me anyway, trusting my vision as he always did.

"What about your riding experience?" Ryan asked.

I told them about my home, which was in Wenatchee (pronounced When-at-chee by the white man), Washington. Its name came from the Wenatchi (also known as P'squosa) people, and it sat at the confluence of the Wenatchee and Columbia Rivers, where the water ran swift and cold, even in summer. Wheat and mustard fields lay to the east, apple orchards stretched to the northern horizon like stitches in an emerald quilt, and the Cascade Mountains towered to the west and south, their peaks crowned with snow, even in July. I rode trails in the canyons, my horse's hooves kicking up dust that smelled of sage and sunbaked earth as we climbed steep hills that led quickly to magnificent views. The kind of views that made you stop breathing for a moment.

"You will be cold. You will be hot. You will be sleeping in tents. You won't always like the food. And there will be chafing. Don't forget chafing. Mongolia will break you. It breaks everyone. And you will still need to get back in the saddle. Can you do that?" Julie asked.

I jumped on this Zoom call immediately after ending a family Zoom call with my sister, who lives on the other side of the state, one daughter who lives across the country, and my other daughter, who lives in my basement. We started our monthly girl Zoom calls when COVID hit. They were waiting to hear how this interview went.

Charlie was in his woodshop, carving wooden spoons that we would later attempt to sell as a fundraiser for the ride. The sweet scent of cherry wood shavings rose around him as he worked, his hands steady despite the constant pain he lived with. He'd already made twelve spoons, each one unique, each one carrying the story of the tree it came from.

I knew what Julie wanted to hear, and I totally believed I was telling the truth when I answered, "Not only can I manage that, the idea of it is thrilling."

Mental mindset is vital to the success of any endurance event. If I had gone then, that very moment, it would have been a very different experience indeed.

The interview lasted about forty-five minutes. When it was done, Julie promised to contact my references. I held my breath for two weeks, jumping every time my phone buzzed, my heart racing whenever I opened my email. And then I got the message. The subject line alone made my hands shake.

I had been accepted!

The interview happened in the spring of 2021. We made plans for that fall, but Charlie passed away two weeks before the scheduled departure. I set the dream aside, not sure I would ever pick it up again. But as the year turned and we neared the anniversary of his passing, I knew I had to do something.

Do Something

Dear Charlie, How am I supposed to blow the waterlines again? And does that have to happen every year? Or can I skip this year? Why didn't I pay attention when you showed me how to work the irrigation pump?

I put down my pen and stared out the window, noticing snowflakes for the first time. Damn. The snow! I forgot about the snow!

The shovel waited in the garage, still bearing the worn grip of his gloved hands. I resented this pristine white blanket of snow I used to find so beautiful, its intrusion of necessary tasks when all I wanted to do was sink into my armchair with his old sweater and his memories.

Dear Charlie, Why did we never buy a snow blower?!

Ugh.

I heaved myself up and forced myself into clothes, and then into snow pants, and then into hat, gloves, scarf, and boots, and trudged outside to deal with this stupid mess.

Vicki, my elderly neighbor, met me outside, worry in her voice. "Rachael, can you get my driveway, too?"

Charlie always took care of her. Did I inherit his neighborhood responsibilities, too?

"Sure," I said, the bitterness boiling. Her grateful response grated on my ears like nails on a chalkboard.

I put away my shovel, drove angrily to the hardware store, bought a snow blower, came home, and immediately accidentally ran over the welcome mat. It twisted up inside the blades, freezing the motor. Damn.

Back inside, my sweet dog Molly, lying in her favorite spot—Charlie's side of the couch—watched me, following me around the room with her brown eyes. Had I fed her today? I couldn't be certain. I filled her bowl just in case. She glanced at it without interest. Maybe I had fed her already? Or maybe she was too sad to eat?

I thought about all the other dumb chores I'd inherited and failed at. I stopped mowing the lawn, which didn't make as much of an impact as you might think, because I also stopped watering it. The grass turned golden, then brown, then disappeared altogether, leaving bare patches of earth that matched how I felt inside—stripped down to nothing but survival.

My horse. My Roan. Not an inherited chore, but so much harder now. I solved that one by hiring an aspiring cowgirl to feed and exercise him. He was in good hands.

Dear Charlie, How is it possible I missed all the tiny things you did for me?

Guilt was flavoring my days sour. I was raw. I was lost. I didn't know what to do. The future looked like a black hole. I could not imagine a tomorrow, let alone a next week, or a next year.

Ride the Gobi Gallop? A small whisper in the air.

What was that?

Ride for miles and miles and never meet a fence. Days that start with sunrise yoga and end with campfire-lit faces that tell stories and sing songs. Laughter and pleasant exhaustion and never-ending views.

The words faded like smoke, leaving me alone again with my to-do list. The day's tasks mocked me: Attend a landscaping class.

I knew nothing about landscaping. Never wanted to. But no

one else was stepping in to do it, and I couldn't afford to hire any-one. So I signed up for a class. I walked in, carrying anger and bit-terness in my backpack next to my notebook.

The first thing the instructor said was, "We are going to go around and introduce ourselves, and I'd like for you to tell us why you signed up for this class."

Why did I sign up? Because my husband died! And now I have to do all these dumb things.

Thankfully, I was not the first to be called. I was in fact last. When she called on me, she said, "Ok, now you, sitting in the back there in the shadows." Did she sense the storm?

"Hi. My name is Rachael Lundin, and I'm just here to learn a little more about creating a no maintenance yard."

My biggest takeaway from the class was there is no such thing as a "no maintenance" yard, which was deeply disappointing.

Was there a way to escape all this? Could it be possible to actu-ally look forward to something?

Dear Charlie, I had a shed delivered today. I need a shed be-cause I need a place to store the lawn mower and the shovel and the snow blower. I can't put them in the garage, obviously. That's where your woodshop is.

I tried to focus on my list. The filters needed replacing in the air conditioners. And in the furnace? Did the furnace have filters? The gutters needed cleaning and there was a brick that had fallen from the chimney. It sat on the roof, accusing me of neglect, and I saw it every time I pulled into the driveway.

I remembered the day I ran out of coffee. Charlie always bought extra coffee. We had cans of it stacked in various corners through-out the house—at least we did, until the day I ran out. I searched everywhere, certain there was another tin. There wasn't. For some reason, looking at my coffee-free cupboards felt like I just lost him all over again. I sank down on the kitchen floor and sobbed.

I looked at my reflection in the window—gray hair escaping its tie, dark circles under my eyes. The woman staring back was a stranger, someone hollow-eyed and uncertain. Not the woman Charlie married, not the one who used to paint and weld and dream. Just a shell trying to remember how to live. Who was I kidding? I could barely manage a snow blower. How could I possibly think about crossing Mongolia on horseback?

"Everything is hard. Might as well make it epic?"

The voice sounded suspiciously like Charlie's. He always pushed me toward adventure while making sure I had solid ground beneath my feet. Now the ground felt like quicksand, each day another slow sink into grief. I picked up my to-do list one more time. The next item mocked me: "Fix the irrigation pump." It turned out that it indeed did need to be blown out every year. Water froze inside it, and when the irrigation water was turned on for the season, I was alerted by the surprise new fountain feature in my front yard.

Somewhere, on the other side of the world, horses ran free across endless steppes, their hooves drumming ancient rhythms into the earth. No pumps to fix. No grass to mow. Just vast sky and endless possibility.

Maybe that was exactly why I should go. If I was going to drown in tasks I couldn't handle, in a life I didn't know how to live anymore, maybe I should at least drown in something magnificent. Something that would make Charlie smile that crooked smile of his and say, "That's my gal."

I looked again at the stranger in the window. For just a moment, I caught a glimpse of something in her eyes, a spark of the woman who once dreamed of adventure. I gave her a tentative smile.

Maybe?

Packing

In all the adventure stories, there is a scene when the hero packs for the journey. I love that scene so much! It's the moment when imagination begins to solidify into reality, when "someday" transforms into "now." Every item chosen is a commitment to the adventure ahead, an acknowledgment that yes, this is really happening. And somehow, in the quiet act of gathering supplies, the hero begins to become the person who will make that journey.

What would I need in Mongolia? I started my packing list when I first decided to go, and I put it on my fridge, where it lived for two years. The first year, Charlie helped add to it, his nearly indecipherable handwriting mixed with mine. He'd add items in his unique phonetic spelling—"waturpruf matchiz," "xtra boot lasis"—items I had to sound out in his hillbilly drawl to understand. This was the man who spelled my name "Ratchel" for years, his internal ear translating everything into his own special dialect. Charlie never graduated high school; a learning disability made reading and writing a constant struggle. He'd get "flustrated" when words didn't come out right, a Charlie-ism that would send the girls into barely suppressed giggles even when, and maybe especially when, he was trying to be serious. Sometimes, now, I have to stop and think which is the correct word—"frustrated" or "flustrated?" But what he lacked in formal education, he made up for in emotional intelligence and practical wisdom. He could read people better than any book, and could sense exactly what someone needed, whether it was a helping hand, a joke, or a "waturpruf jackit" added to their packing list.

The second year, his additions were buried beneath refrigerator magnets holding higher-priority items like plumber and electrician contacts and repair services, and how-to classes that I resented attending and appreciated at the same time.

I excavated it about a month before the trip, peeling away layers of Post-its and business cards like an archaeologist uncovering artifacts from another life. Charlie's suggestions were still there, waiting patiently beneath it all, his handwriting unchanged while everything else had shifted.

I laid out my life for the next two weeks: layers for four seasons in one suitcase, emergency medications, a below-zero sleeping bag, and, incongruously, a floor-length gala gown. Every ounce was precious with the fifty-pound weight limit. In the end, space constraints forced impossible choices—my big camera and helmet didn't make the cut, decisions I would later regret.

One thing I knew in the few days before I left: I was going to be facing a challenging journey, and my tolerance for challenging was at an all-time low. So, if it had the potential to reduce the stress load, I tried to force it in.

My living room looked like it had been ransacked by a very particular burglar who only wanted wool socks and moisture-wicking base layers. Rejected items with price tags still attached lay scattered across the floor like fallen soldiers.

Killing Time

As I left the house, I looked at Charlie's picture and answered all the questions he would have been asking me. "Yep, I have my charger. Meds are packed. Underwear and socks—got 'em. Passport and credit cards. Got my cash. Anything else? Oh, that's right, my brush!"

The first major stop on my Mongolian journey was a twenty-four-hour layover in Seoul, where I learned my first lesson about traveling alone: how to make an adventure out of waiting. In that giant airport, I discovered pockets of wonder: a musician playing an ajaeng, a Korean bowed string instrument, its plunking slippery tones strange to my Western ears, making me feel already far from home. I joined children at a cultural craft station, learning how to make a traditional Korean paper *ddakji* from thick paper, tucking the finished product into my carry-on as a future gift for my granddaughter. When night fell, I found sleep on a surprisingly comfortable bench, my belt looped through my luggage handles, a traveler's trick to deter theft while attempting a peaceful rest.

Twenty-four hours in an airport changes you. By hour twenty, even the most patient traveler develops sharp edges. I found my gate for the final flight to Ulaanbaatar, my nerves frayed from too much fluorescent light and too little sleep. But, even if I had been well-rested, I think I would have been irritated when a group of men passed, one physically pushing me aside, to get on the plane. I swallowed my protests, too tired to care, and confident that, in this big world, I would not have to deal with their arrogance again. I focused instead on the luxury of my exit-row seat with blessed extra legroom.

I stretched out, preparing to enjoy this last moment of comfort before the wildness of my destination, but my peaceful bubble kept being pierced by movement in my peripheral vision: The largest of the men, the one who had pushed me, crammed into a seat a row behind and across. The headrest hit him between his shoulder blades, his knees pressed against his chest. This man was NBA basketball player tall, with an extra hundred pounds. I thought how uncomfortable he must be, all the time. Everywhere he went, the world would be too small. Constantly forced into confined spaces. Constantly making allowances. Those things will wear you out. Even the best of us can become jerks with that kind of consistent existence.

I tried to ignore him. Tried to remind myself that rudeness shouldn't be rewarded. But watching him fold himself smaller and smaller, discomfort etched in every line of his face...

When I turned to offer my seat, his expression shifted from irritation (another stranger bothering him) to blank disbelief to pure gratitude. In that moment of surrender to compassion, I made an unexpected friend. For the rest of the flight, I learned about his quest to catch a fish species found nowhere else on Earth but Mongolia's rivers.

I arrived in Ulaanbaatar a full week early, knowing that jet lag and exhaustion were enemies I could at least try to control.

My introduction to Ulaanbaatar came in the backseat of a battered Honda Civic, sharing space with a six-year-old boy who treated the car like his personal gymnasium. After a mix-up sent my driver to the wrong airport, she'd burst through the arrival doors, forty-five minutes late, flustered and apologetic. Driving people around was her side hustle, but she was still a mom, with mother responsibilities. Her daughter claimed the front seat while her son and I took the back. No one wore seatbelts. As the boy performed impromptu push-ups, his feet propped against the back window, his hands braced on the front headrests, we wound through streets that seemed to circle back on themselves endlessly. Soviet-era apartment blocks loomed like giant concrete dominoes, their stark, gray faces softened here and there by bright murals and satellite dishes. Between them, glass-fronted luxury hotels reached skyward, while at their feet, traditional *gers* tucked into vacant lots like mushrooms sprouting through cracks in the sidewalk. My confidence in reaching the correct hotel wavered with each familiar-looking corner we passed.

When we finally arrived at my hotel overlooking Chinggis Khan (another name for Genghis Khan) Square, I stepped out on wobbly legs, equal parts relieved and exhilarated. Ulaanbaatar, I was learning, was a city where horses walked freely down the streets between cars packed bumper to bumper, where a twenty-five-minute walk became an hour-long drive, and where traffic was so bad they'd implemented a complicated system allowing only odd or even license plates on alternating days. A city of contrasts, where the old and new, traditional and modern, order and chaos all coexist in a kind of chaotic harmony.

I spent the first day relying upon Julie Veloo's hospitality to dictate my agenda, like an insecure teenager who finds making her own doctor appointments intimidating. The dependency made me squirm, so on day two, I put aside my insecurity and ventured out into the city with just my translation app. My foreignness was impossible to disguise, but joining crowd flows at intersections and haggling with leather-working street artists created at least an illusion of competence.

I already had regrets about my packing choices, so I decided to fix that. The purchase of an overpriced camera became my first solo victory in this strange city.

Julie arranged a tour of the school we were raising money for, a building with its own story of survival and transformation. The original structure, a donated office building, had come with a catch: Move it in one week or lose it. Through the magic that is Mongolia, Julie told me, they'd somehow made it happen. But the school's success created new challenges as more children needed space. The solution came in the form of a three-story addition made from stacked shipping containers—practical, if not pretty. Still, there was beauty in its purpose: Every recycled container meant more children had a safe place to learn.

For some reason, I was nervous about this visit. Standing in front of this testament to Julie's determination, this patchwork building that refused to apologize for its appearance because it was too busy serving its purpose, I wasn't sure how to act or what was expected of me. I clutched my offering—three large packages of craft pipe cleaners—in sweaty hands.

I bought these because they were light and fit in my luggage, and I wanted to bring something. I figured these could be added to the art supplies for later use. Instead, the lovely ladies sat all the children in a circle and then asked me to teach them what to do with pipe cleaners. All eyes turned to me! Suddenly, I had stage fright!

Lucky for me, pipe cleaners were one of my favorite fidget toys. My nervous fingers found comfort in the familiar twist and bend of the wires. Soon, small hands joined mine, mimicking each motion, creating a rainbow of necklaces, rings, bracelets, and silly glasses. The children's laughter needed no translation, their delight erasing some of my awkwardness. In their joy, I caught a glimpse of why Julie had created this place, why this mattered so much.

Coming early had been a good idea to get acclimated, but this time of waiting also forced me to face the immensity of what I'd signed up for. My internal panic waxed and waned like the moon over the city, but it never quite disappeared. In those quiet moments of doubt, I could hear Charlie's voice as clearly as if he were beside me: "Sometimes, the only way out is through it." He'd said it after his accident, during his recovery, and now his words were guiding me through my own journey of becoming.

3

Mongolia!

My To-Do List

"Mongolian ponies, who spend months running free on the steppe, live and die by their herd instinct. Fall behind while riding, and you'll discover this truth the hard way—either your horse bolts in blind panic, galloping breakneck through any obstacle to rejoin its herd, or worse, freezes completely, refusing to move another step alone in the vastness."

It was three days before the ride, and Julie Veloo was sharing her words of wisdom with me over coffee in the mall. It was a warm Mongolian day, and we were in clean, comfortable clothes, sitting at a table in a busy coffee shop, where the familiar smell of espresso fought with unfamiliar food aromas. Her words about bolting horses and panic runs settled like stones in my stomach, each scenario adding weight to my growing anxiety.

She continued, "I had that happen to me once. And it was awful. I was in tears, trying to get going. And it was way past dark before I finally made it to camp."

I pictured the terrifying scenario, wandering the Mongolian Steppe in pitch blackness with a terrified pony. Alone. Lost. I gave myself a little shake and returned to the present.

Meeting Julie was like meeting a celebrity. I had read her

words, watched her YouTube videos, and I'd seen the Gobi Gallop documentary. She was just as engaging in person, her gray hair cropped short, her skin weathered by countless hours under the Mongolian sun. She walked briskly with a stiff-legged limp, but her energy radiated like a force field. I found myself almost jogging to keep up with her through the mall corridors.

Julie had to go to the mall to pick up some items for the trek, and she invited me to meet her there. I was the only rider yet to arrive, and she was being an excellent hostess by showing me as much of Ulaanbaatar as she had time for.

"We're a small team this year," Julie said over her coffee, her eyes crinkling with a mix of pride and concern. "Covid canceled our 2020 ride completely. Last year, I rode solo. And now..." She gestured at the geopolitical realities—a world still grappling with pandemic uncertainties, the new tensions with Russia and China casting shadows over this land caught between powers. "You all really are the intrepid few."

"How different is this from your usual rides?" I asked.

"Usually we ride in June—longer days, lusher grass. The horses have more time to graze; we have more daylight for rest breaks. September..." She shook her head. "We'll have to push harder, cover the same ground in fewer daylight hours. And then there's the cold." She smiled. "But that's why you're here, isn't it? For the challenge?"

Before I could answer, we were approached by a businessman in a crisp suit and a woman in a tailored dress. Julie introduced me as "one of the intrepid Gobi Gallop riders." And then they sized me up.

I thought I looked the part. I was in jeans and I had on my cold-weather boots. I was wearing my fleece top, and my gray hair was in twin French braids, which I had to learn how to do when my girls were in high school sports. I always felt tougher when my hair was braided.

They offered words of encouragement and admiration. I felt like a fake, but I smiled and nodded.

My mind was all internal panic. *What have I done? How is it possible that I'm actually here?* I added "Stay with the group" to my to-do list for when I was out on the ride and I smiled at the people with counterfeit confidence.

"Those Mongolian ponies aren't like our horses!" A woman back home told me before I left. "You're likely to get bucked off a couple times." She emphasized the word "you're" as if to say that I was definitely going to get bucked off.

I've only been bucked off once, and that wasn't a bad experience at all. The horse's name was Willow, and she tended to buck when asked to change gait. I knew that, but somehow believed she wouldn't do that with me—that special brand of rider overconfidence that comes right before a lesson in humility. I was wrong. I went over her right shoulder and landed on my butt.

"The ground will always catch you," my stepfather, Bud, used to say. And now I knew it was true.

I got back on her and kept riding. I wasn't hurt, and I felt pretty good about the whole thing. It wasn't until later that I felt scared of her. A delayed reaction.

I repeated my internal list.

- Stay with the group.
- Don't get bucked off.

I followed Julie around while she was shopping. I was feeling very nervous. It occurred to me that I could tell them I changed my mind. I could stay in my hotel the whole time. Safe, uninjured...bored.

Nope, I couldn't do that. I might die out there, cold and miserable, but the thought of not going seemed worse.

So I said, "Tell me about the saddles we are riding."

"They are a sort of cross between English and Western," Julie answered.

I was having trouble picturing this. I had only ridden English once, and I was not comfortable. I was used to Western. I like the solidness of the saddle. There was plenty to grip and hold on to.

Western saddles were for work—herding cows, roping steers, long trail rides with saddle bags. They were meant for all-day riding for multiple days. In my mind, English saddles were for performance. Jumping, dressage, and playing. They were lightweight and didn't come with a built-in handle.

"A cross between a Western and an English saddle" sounded to me like something you say to make both types of riders feel like there is hope that whatever they ride, there will be something they will be familiar with on this saddle. It did not bring me comfort.

I was going to ride wild horses on equipment I was not familiar with. I was seriously questioning my sanity. The mall suddenly felt too warm, too crowded. My anxiety had its own shopping list: more toilet paper and extra chap stick. Each item was a tiny attempt to control something, anything, in this endless unknown I was walking into.

Western Saddle

I had one potential friend here in Mongolia, Daniel Miller. I met him online, specifically through the Gobi Gallop Facebook page. Daniel Miller had spent his career living and working in Mongolia for the Peace Corps, the UN, and sometimes, he came just for fun. He was the kind of person whose life sounds like a movie plot: cowboy, photographer, scientist, and saddle collector, splitting his time between Wyoming and Mongolia.

He was in Mongolia and, more importantly, in Ulaanbaatar, at the same time I was. Two days before the ride, he asked me if I wanted to meet for coffee.

I said "Yes!" then immediately thought, *And that was the last anyone saw of Rachael Lundin.* Years of crime shows had taught me to be wary, especially as a woman alone in a country where I didn't even know how to call emergency services. But after weighing the risks, I pocketed my multitool (a.k.a. self-defense weapon) and headed down to meet this Daniel Miller, who could be exactly who he claimed to be, or a part-time serial killer in a country where hiding a body would be extremely easy.

He met me in my hotel lobby, and we recognized each other right away. The late-afternoon sun slanted through the windows, catching the silver in his bushy mustache that overhung his smile. His blue eyes peered through round gold-and-black-rimmed glasses, set in a face weathered by years under both Wyoming and Mongolian skies. He wore a white wide-brimmed hat, a button-down jean shirt, blue jeans, and cowboy boots, looking exactly like what he was: an American cowboy who'd found his second home in Mongolia.

"Hello, Rachael," he said. "Nice to finally meet you in person!"

We went to the coffee shop inside my hotel at his suggestion. I really appreciated that. Did he suspect I was a scared rabbit, ready to bolt?

Over lattes by the window, I said, "So, the Peace Corps?"

His weathered face lit up. "This country gets in your blood," he said, gesturing at the city beyond the window. "But it's changing so fast." He described how the shrinking grasslands were forcing nomadic families into Ulaanbaatar, creating a cascade of challenges. Generations of herding knowledge didn't translate to city jobs. Families who'd lived freely on the steppe found themselves cramped in ger districts, struggling with poverty, addiction, domestic violence—problems not unique to Mongolia, but amplified by the rapid pace of change.

"The environmental impact is just as concerning," he continued, his hands wrapped around his cooling coffee. "Overgrazing weakens the land, turns it to desert. We're losing about 1,300 square miles of grazing land every year."

"Can anything be done?" I asked.

He smiled, but it didn't reach his eyes. "That's complicated. Mongolians have a deep national pride in their problem-solving skills. Sometimes that pride, that hubris, makes them resistant to outside suggestions."

Something about this sparked a deeper understanding in me. Like grief, I thought, some journeys can only be walked by those experiencing them. Others can offer support, but true healing has to come from within. Maybe Mongolia would find its own solutions—not despite its pride but because of it.

I didn't share these thoughts with Daniel. They felt too new and unformed.

And then the conversation turned to the upcoming ride. "So, you have riding experience, right?" Daniel asked.

And what he was really asking was, *Am I capable of taking on a 700K ride done in ten riding days?*

And I wondered, *am I?*

Which was closely followed by the thought, *No! You have gotten in way over your head. You are going to die.*

Out loud I said the thing I'd practiced: "Oh, yes. I grew up with horses. My parents were ropers, and we had our own arena for that purpose. But I prefer trail rides. I enjoy getting out and seeing the countryside."

Maybe he sensed my unease because he asked me more questions. "Do you know what saddle you will ride in?"

"They are Russian military surplus saddles. They are a sort of cross between Western and English. But I haven't seen one yet."

And here was where Daniel Miller changed the course of my entire adventure.

"I have a saddle," he said, and those four words changed everything. Hope rose in my chest as he continued. "It's a Western saddle."

The saddle, he explained, was made in the 1950s, smaller than modern Western saddles, which means that it fit the smaller horses here. "You should take it on your ride."

"Really?" the word came out breathless. What a relief it would be that in this new and strange environment, I could ride in at least one thing that was familiar.

"Yes, really. You tell Julie I said you could ride in my saddle. As a matter of fact, I'll tell her." And he pulled out his phone and emailed her right then.

And so it was on the first day of the ride, while everyone mounted up in Russian Military Surplus or traditional Mongolian saddles, and I swung into a familiar Western saddle. It was the only thing about that day that wouldn't feel foreign. When all else went to hell, I knew I could at least hold on to a solid saddle horn.

I'm really glad Daniel turned out to be exactly what he claimed to be. Mongolia might have a lot of places to hide a body—endless steppes, remote mountains, vast desert—but it would have been a hassle to deal with that before going on the Gobi Gallop. I would have had to hire a driver, find a shovel, navigate the language barrier to buy quicklime...honestly, who had time for murder when there's a 700-kilometer ride to prepare for?

Meeting the Team

Not everyone is like you, and that's OK. You do you. When you do, you will find yourself in situations that only people like you find themselves in, and that's where you meet your tribe.

When I was saying goodbye to my friends before the trip, they teased me about meeting someone and falling in love. Of course, I was way ahead of them. I promised myself to be single for a year, just to give me time to get my head straight. A year seemed like a good amount of time. Hadn't I heard that advice somewhere? Don't make any big decisions for at least a year after something like this. It translated to my mind that after a year, I would be ready. But that year was up, and I didn't feel ready, but *maybe* it was time to start looking? Maybe "ready" depended on meeting the right person?

The Gobi Gallop was funded in part by the riders' fundraising efforts, which the facilitators helped with by creating online profiles for each rider. People who donate can go to their favorite rider's profile and donate directly.

Each profile included photos of the riders and a bio, as well as information about the school. It was also a nice way for us to get to know whom we would be riding with.

I, however, read through each of their profiles with an eye toward potential matches. Would I be finding love in Mongolia? It didn't take long for me to find my answer.

I met Brandon first. He also came a few days early. When I researched Brandon, I learned he was from New Zealand, he worked in artificial intelligence, and he had an office in Washington State, so there was a chance I'd get to see him after this was all done. And I knew that one thing he had on his agenda that day was to give a lecture at the local university. This all sounded very impressive on paper. In person, he was a bundle of perpetual motion, words tumbling out between quick hand-gestures, his excitement about the upcoming university lecture making him practically vibrate. His energy filled the cab like static electricity, and I found myself instinctively leaning back, creating space between us as I tried to process this human whirlwind. He was almost too much for me.

We all went to visit the school, and this time Julie gave us the official tour. We saw the sewing center, where we got a peek at the gifts Julie had specially ordered for the team. And then Brandon and I were delivered to a classroom, a different one from when I came earlier that week, where we were encouraged to play with the children. My pipe cleaners were brought out again. I got pictures this time.

We went to a second classroom, where they had a surprise for us. It was a dance they had been working on. Brandon jumped in and danced with them, his long limbs moving with surprising grace as he mimicked the children's movements. All the other adults watched from the side, our backs pressed against colorful classroom walls. I wasn't sure if Brandon regretted his decision to join the kids. Sweat showed through his shirt while his initial confidence seemed to waver. The dance went on longer than expected—but he was committed now, and he saw it through to the end, earning delighted giggles from his young partners.

This jumping in and being committed was reflected in how Brandon seemed to approach everything. For example, I learned that he had only started riding in January of that year; he'd decided to do the Gobi Gallop first, and second took on the challenge of learning to ride.

He'd found a stable in New Zealand and committed to an intensive training schedule with a strict Russian instructor who demanded perfection in every movement and every position. In nine months, he'd logged more hours on horseback than the rest of us combined, though not more than our collective lifetime experience. I admired and worried about this approach in equal measure: Was intensive training enough preparation for what lay ahead?

The third classroom was the one I visited earlier that week; they all remembered me and treated me like their class pet. I kinda loved it. We colored together.

While I was coloring, I felt Charlie looking over my shoulder, and then I saw him in my memory befriending a child in Tanzania with crayons we brought with us and a coloring book we found in the market. I smiled at him. The moment felt bright and happy.

The final classroom we visited was the toddler class, and it was chaos in there. One child was falling asleep where she stood, another was trying to climb up the wall to reach some paper towels. The two instructors were grateful for our extra hands.

All these kids, every single one of them, was a refugee from the city garbage dump. We toured the kitchens where their healthy meals were prepared. We saw the library where they and their older siblings could spend after-school hours, but I was starting to understand that "school" was too simple a word for what Julie had created here. The building pulsed with multiple purposes; seamstresses recruited from the community learned their trade in one room, while parents trained for office jobs in another. The library wasn't just for students; it was a community hub, its doors open to anyone seeking knowledge or just a warm place to read. Even the kitchen served a dual purpose—not just feeding children but training future food-service workers. Each room seemed to say, "Here is another way out." The school wasn't just educating children; it was lifting entire families out of poverty, one skill at a time. As we learned about the plans for expansion, I was humbled to be a part of this project. This wasn't charity; it was transformation on a scale I hadn't imagined when I first signed up to ride across Mongolia.

A love connection? At the end of the day, I decided Brandon was not a match for me. I probably decided that in the first few minutes. He was too young (he would say I was too old). In fact, later in the ride, he referred to me as "Mother." Nope, there would be no love connection between Brandon and me.

Charlie would have laughed at me assessing everyone's romantic potential. I'd never been one to scan rooms for potential partners. Charlie had simply happened to me, like sunrise happens to morning. But here I was, taking inventory of hearts like I was shopping for shoes. Maybe checking for love connections was just easier than examining what I was really searching for out here.

Finally, I was back in my hotel for one more night. I repacked everything, sorting what would stay in Ulaanbaatar and what would go on the trek. I would meet the rest of my team in the morning. It was a long time before I went to sleep.

The next morning, I walked into the breakfast area of my hotel and saw Haven sitting at a table. We recognized each other immediately

Haven stood to shake my hand, and I asked if I could join him for breakfast.

"Of course!"

Haven had dark brown hair, and he was somewhere around six feet tall. He was wearing a blue t-shirt and jeans that looked comfortable rather than carefully chosen. I noted that he was my age—the kind of detail that matters when you're sizing up potential connections, even if you're trying not to.

One of Haven's pictures on his donations profile was of him on a horse standing on a boulder, and the horse seemed to be considering stepping onto the next boulder. It was impressive. Haven said that the picture was taken when he rode with Julie on the Ride to the Reindeer. The Ride to the Reindeer was one of several rides offered by Horse Trek Mongolia. Their website describes it like this:

"This once-in-a-lifetime ride will take you across 3000-meter-high mountains, along the shores of the famed lake Khovsgul and up to meet the Tsataan Peoples—the last surviving truly nomadic Reindeer tribe on the planet."

Oh, so he has been here before. He knows what to expect, I thought.

He had a bag of pills, which he was a little embarrassed about. He said the people back home, his eastern medicine friends, stocked him up for every possible ailment, and we talked a little about the eastern approach to medicine.

He shared he taught Tai Chi.

Tai Chi? I remembered my visions of yoga at sunrise. Tai Chi was even better. How often did he practice Tai Chi? Daily. I locked that in right then and there with, "Would it be OK if I joined you?"

Yes, that would be OK. Maybe even welcome.

He talked about previous journeys he had taken and the sicknesses people experienced: mountain sickness, elevation sickness, food poisoning, and other travel sicknesses. These things were common, especially if you add physical exertion into the mix. But with medications, he had successfully avoided the sicknesses while all his travel companions suffered.

I listened in awe. The Gobi Gallop documentary showed a year when the whole team got sick with something. It was sounding like this could be a real possibility for me, too, and I worried I wasn't prepared enough in that way. It was too late for any more panic-buying. What I had was going to have to be enough.

When you meet someone for the first time, there is all this surface stuff going on—the words you say, the physical movements you make. But there are things going on under the surface, too. Things that I don't have words for. A communication that happens on a soul-level.

With Haven, my soul said to me, *Here is someone worth knowing.*

A love connection? No. But I recognized immediately that I had a friend. Love has many faces.

After breakfast, I went to my room, grabbed all my luggage, and hauled it down to the lobby. A driver would come to pick up four of us there, and then we would go get Brandon at his hotel, and finally Carly. When I arrived in the lobby, I immediately picked out Tom.

Tom was dressed in military fatigues, the fabric worn in places that spoke of actual use rather than fashion. His gray hair matched his gray beard, and he was focused on making sure all his things were packed with the kind of precision that suggested old habits die hard. He didn't make eye contact, and his movements were economical and purposeful, every gesture saying, "I have a job to do here, and socializing ain't it."

I had learned from Julie that he was our medic. She said about Tom, "He doesn't have the nicest bedside manner. He's more likely to respond to complaints with a 'What did you expect was going to happen?'" So I was mentally prepared to be as tough as possible when Tom was around. No whining and complaining from me. Not that I would do that, anyway.

This was what I learned about Tom that first day: He was from Northern Ireland, and he spent some time in South Africa. He was former military, which was where he earned his field medic credentials. He said "Fuck" a lot.

Later, while riding in the van, he emphasized that he was "Not a doctor." He didn't want to be sued. But he promised he could take care of us, up to and including *removing* any crushed limbs.

This was not as reassuring as you might think.

There was general silence after he'd made that statement. I imagined varying degrees of panic. I know my thought was, *Wait, crushed limbs are a possibility?* Followed by, *Of course it is a possibility, you dummy.* So I said out loud, "I think probably I will be fine with you *not* removing any crushed limbs. I can hold out until you get me to a hospital."

"Me, too," said Haven and Brandon.

I don't remember Carly's response. She might have been sleeping.

I added "Don't crush any limbs" to my list.

A love connection? Tom was in my age group. He was strong and capable. But he was also married, and when he talked about her, I knew he had already found his perfect fit.

The other person in the hotel lobby was Ashley. He was weighed down by several camera equipment bags. I didn't have any pre-knowledge of Ashley, so I was starting from scratch with him. I noted light-brown hair and a neatly trimmed brown beard. He said he was to be our videographer. He planned to ride in the van with us, interviewing us, taking footage, and he was going to ride with us on our first day. After that, he would return to Ulaanbaatar and prepare for when we crossed the finish line.

I learned Ashley had a vlog, *Simple Wild Living*.

He admired my camera, and we discussed lenses. My knowledge of terms was pretty limited, but I felt validated that I had a good setup.

I liked Ashley's accent; it was new to me. I learned it was South African.

Ashley was also the videographer for the Blue-Wolf Totem ride.

Ahh, the Blue-Wolf Totem. I was a little jealous of the Blue-Wolf Totem. Before the Blue-Wolf, the Gobi Gallop was the longest charity ride on the planet. But then here came the Blue-Wolf Totem ride—three months in Mongolia. That was tough to beat, and impossible for someone who must maintain employment. Suddenly, the Gobi Gallop didn't seem so cool. But I consoled myself that we were still the longest *annual* charity ride.

Ashley shared that he had seen what people look like before and after a ride, and he told us to appreciate our current clean and shiny state.

A love connection? Nope. Ashley was too young for me and married. Were any of these men going to be single?

The four of us—Tom, Ashley, Haven, and I—were picked up in a van, and we headed down the street to Brandon's hotel. He was outside and ready for us. And soon Carly arrived in a different car.

I was worried about Carly before I ever met her. Her original flight was canceled, so her arrival was delayed until the morning of our twelve-hour drive. Between flights, layovers, and time changes, she was already arriving exhausted. But she didn't want to inconvenience anyone and told Julie, "Just send me the GPS coordinates and I'll figure out a way to the starting line."

Just send her the GPS coordinates? I was in awe. I worried to the point of obsessing about every part of my travel. I even arrived several days early so that I could get used to the time change. Here was a young woman with enough travel experience to have the confidence to say, "Just send me the GPS coordinates." And now that I know Carly better, I believe she could have indeed figured it all out.

But, of course, we didn't let that happen. Julie arranged for her to be picked up and brought to a hotel, where she had maybe three hours of sleep, and then brought her to join us in the van for the twelve-hour drive.

What I knew about Carly was pretty limited. Her pictures showed she had done show jumping. In person, she was lean and strong, her hair pulled back in an efficient ponytail, the kind of practical style that suggested she valued function over form. She smiled her huge smile—the kind that usually lit up her whole face, I would later learn—but now her eyes weren't entirely focused, like she was operating on autopilot through a fog of jet lag. Later she would say she barely remembered that drive. She held her own in conversation with the determination of someone used to pushing through discomfort, but finally, she gave in and slept, her head bobbing against the van window while Mongolia's landscape rolled past. I was so glad she wasn't alone and trying to navigate Mongolia.

Later, when we all fell apart from exhaustion, remember this: Carly started the ride, exhausted. The rest of us had at least one night's sleep under our belts, and I had an entire week to get acclimated. When pushing limits, it is the little things that can make the difference.

A love connection? Yes! Carly and I connected immediately. When someone can read an entire comedy routine in your raised eyebrow—part slapstick, part gallows humor—and respond with a shrug that somehow manages to say "I know, right?" and "We're all going to die" and "But isn't it kind of hilarious?" all at once, you've found more than a friend. You've found someone who gets the cosmic joke of it all, how something can be both the hardest thing you've ever done and the most ridiculous situation you've ever been in. These silent conversations became our secret language of survival, equal parts commiseration and comedy. Not a love connection in the way I'd been cataloging them, but maybe something even more precious.

The van itself became our first shared experience, a well-worn vehicle with seats that had carried countless other adventurers before us. Tom claimed the front passenger seat without discussion, his medical kit always within easy reach. Haven and I settled into the back row, while Brandon squeezed into the middle with Ashley and his camera equipment. The morning sun slanted through dusty windows as we navigated Ulaanbaatar's chaotic traffic, each of us stealing glances at one another, trying to gauge who these strangers were that we'd be depending on for the next ten days.

When Carly joined us, she brought a shift in the energy, fresh exhaustion meeting our nervous excitement. The van rearranged itself to accommodate her, Ashley's camera gear shifting, bodies sliding over to make space. The interior filled with that particular awkwardness of strangers forced into intimate proximity, all of us trying to find the balance between friendly and overwhelming while we settled in.

We humans have personal bubbles, invisible barriers we know not to cross. In some cultures, these bubbles are smaller, in others, bigger. And when barriers are crossed, you notice it. On the van ride out, when we were first getting to know one another, it was crowded, luggage piled all over the place, and bodies needing to unfold. For mutual comfort, we gave away those precious inches to one another, legs touching as we stretched out, and shoulders touching as we relaxed.

When we left the city behind, our different personalities began to emerge in how we handled the transition. Tom kept his eyes forward, occasionally offering gruff commentary about the medical supplies he'd brought, each word carrying the weight of experience. Haven maintained a calm presence, his Tai Chi practitioner's serenity a counterpoint to Brandon's continuous stream of enthusiasm.

The landscape outside transformed from urban chaos to endless emptiness, but inside our van, a different change was taking place: individuals slowly becoming a team. Conversation ebbed and flowed naturally. Sometimes we'd all fall silent, lost in our own thoughts about what lay ahead. Other times, someone would share a joke or observation that would pull us back together. Even Carly, fighting sleep, would occasionally contribute a surprisingly witty comment before her eyes would drift closed again.

I found myself watching them all, memorizing details: the way Tom's accent got stronger when he talked about medical emergencies; how Haven's hands moved in small, controlled gestures while he spoke; Brandon's infectious laugh; Ashley's quiet observations; and Carly's determined effort to stay engaged despite her exhaustion. These people would be my whole world for the next ten days, and I was already starting to care about each of them in different ways.

Facebook Post: The Day Before the Ride

Woke up with the soundtrack from the *Man from Snowy River* in my head. That scene where all the cowboys are gathered in the yard, getting ready to chase the Brumbies (Wild horses). Lots of excitement in that scene!

I am not sure what my signal situation will be, but keep an eye on the Gobi Gallop page! They will do Facebook live events and postings with our real-time GPS link.

4

Day One

Excitement

Date: September 11, 2022
Distance: 47K or 30 miles

The morning air still carried the night's chill, but the rising sun promised heat to come, its rays catching the frost on the grass tips and turning them to diamonds.

Above us, the sky opened up in that particular Mongolian way that made me understand why they call it the Land of the Eternal Blue Sky—a dome so vast and deep it seems to swallow you whole. No trees interrupted the view and no buildings blocked the wind that swept across the plain, bringing with it the scent of sage and dust and adventure.

Steam rose from coffee cups clutched in nervous hands while we gathered around the horses. Their coats were already thickening in preparation for winter. These sturdy descendants of Genghis Khan's war mounts watched us with knowing eyes. That's when someone noticed my saddle.

"OK, why does Rachael get a Western saddle?"

I opened my mouth to answer, but Carly beat me to it, her

53

exhaustion from yesterday replaced by mischievous energy. "Because Rachael romanced a man into letting her use his saddle."

And I smiled because I already liked her version of the story much more than mine. The leather of Daniel's saddle gleamed in the early light, its familiar shape standing out among the angular Russian Army surplus saddles being distributed.

"Oh, really?" asked Brandon, his New Zealand accent making it is sound more like *Oh Rilly?* "How'd she do that?"

And the story took on a life of its own, growing more outrageous with each contribution. I tossed in "I met him on the internet!" while Haven and others volunteered increasingly ridiculous details: "She revealed her wrists!" "There was some ankle showing, too!" "Oh yeah, she worked it."

I was laughing too hard to dispute any of it, the anxious first-day-of-the-ride nerves breaking like a fever. Beside me, Carly's eyes danced with mirth, though I could see her hands fidgeting with her riding gloves. We'd already confided in each other, whispering our shared fear of being the worst riders the Mongolian Steppe had ever seen. We shared nervous glances throughout the morning prep, our earlier laughter a thin disguise for our anxiety.

The mood shifted as Zulaa, son of Baagii and Saraa, approached with an enormous box. He was a young man whose smile seemed permanently etched on his face, unable to complete any task without teasing someone. He staggered dramatically under the box's weight, earning eye rolls from his parents and chuckles from the group. Then he stood beside it, attempting and failing to look serious as Julie gathered us all—riders, guides, and support crew—for the official welcome to the 9th Annual Gobi Gallop.

The morning sun climbed higher, and with it, our anticipation. Soon we would be matching riders to horses, and all this nervous energy would have somewhere to go. But for now, we stood in a circle, drinking coffee gone cold, waiting to begin the adventure we'd all traveled so far to find.

Meeting the Crew

This was my first good look at the crew that would be helping to make sure we survived this ride. They stood in a loose circle, their shadows stretching long across the frost-tipped grass, each of them as much a part of this landscape as the endless horizon behind them.

Our primary guide was Baagii, whom I'd seen in the documentary, though he was much more intimidating in person. He reminded me of a Mongolian Clint Eastwood, standing with one boot propped on a rock, his weathered *deel* coat moving in the wind. His steely eyes surveyed the horizon with a cigarette at his lip, seeming to read the vast emptiness like a familiar book. He appeared to care not one whit for human comfort. He was all about the horses, his gaze following their movements with an intensity that made me both grateful for and slightly terrified of his expertise.

Our rear guide was a sweet, smiling man whose name I struggled to pronounce. It sounded to me like Tsloulga, but I learned later it was spelled Lhaagva. He smiled, and it reminded me so strongly of Charlie's kindness and compassion that it comforted me. He was standing with his wife, Tuya, both of them at ease in this empty vastness that made the rest of us feel so small.

Bayaraa was the driver of the medic van and sometimes he was our camera operator. He stood about my height—compact and solid, with black hair and strong square features. He wasn't overly expressive, but his steady watchfulness and quiet friendliness made it clear he was looking out for us, whether that meant driving the van or expertly handling the camera equipment that documented our journey.

Ashley was there, getting film coverage. He already had shots of the crew rounding up the horses. We watched, entranced, as one spunky black horse who wasn't in the mood to be caught, but also unwilling to travel far without his friends, pranced in wide circles. He gave a merry chase around and around our camp, his hooves drumming a rhythm on the hard earth, until one guide's rope finally found its mark. The horse's antics felt like a preview of the wildness awaiting us out there on the steppe.

We weren't formally introduced to the rest of the crew, but they stood there as witnesses to these events. There was the tall, handsome man with a perpetually worried face, whom I learned later was our chef, recruited for this adventure by Zulaa. His presence promised warm meals in cold places. Then there was the man whose face we never saw, not once throughout the entire trip, at least not that we knew of. He wore a ski mask ALL THE TIME. At first, we all guessed that he was worried about Covid. But we learned later that he was worried about the sun darkening his skin. The ugly stigma against dark skin was here in Mongolia, too. And then there were four or five others that my overexcited mind couldn't quite attach memorable characteristics to, but I knew they were there, their presence as constant and natural as the wind that swept across the plain.

Any love connections? Nope. All are married as far as I can tell. It seemed like this would be a romance-less trip. But maybe that was OK?

Deels

Julie reached into the box that Zulaa had dramatically hauled over and pulled out a garment called a *deel*. A deel was a traditional item of clothing worn by both men and women for centuries among Mongols, Turkic, and Tungusic peoples. It was like a caftan or tunic—think overcoat with centuries of nomadic wisdom built in. They typically reached down to the wearer's knees and fanned out at the bottom, the design perfect for both riding and walking. Instead of buttoning down the middle, the sides were pulled against the wearer's body like an embrace—the right flap was close to the body, and the left covered it. On the right side of the garment there were typically five or six hooks to hold the top flap in place. A silk sash typically formed a belt around the middle.

Julie had ours custom made. She chose thick fabrics—a rough, royal blue fabric that reminded me of blue jeans for the outside, soft flannel for the inside—in anticipation of the cold winter days predicted for the end of our ride. Our names were embroidered in gold on the right sleeve and the fabric layers were quilted together.

She called us forward to receive them. And then we began what felt like a clothing ceremony. It took a team to get us secured in our deels—the complicated buttons and the long silk sash required multiple hands and laughter as we stood, arms akimbo, like royalty with our team of valets.

My deel had six hooks total: one at the neck, two on the right shoulder, one under my right armpit, and two on my right hip, each one securing me against the wind that never stops blowing across the steppe. Our sashes, or belts, were of shimmering golden silk. The area between the flaps and above the belt formed a large pocket in which the wearer could store objects.

Julie then demonstrated one very useful feature of a deel: its ability to provide cover for when nature calls. The steppe was a wide open place. I mean, seriously wide open. Miles and miles of nothing but grass and sky meeting at a horizon that seemed to mock the very concept of privacy. And our little camp had a surprising amount of eyes, so it was very difficult to head off in any direction without being seen. I had already spent a ridiculous amount of time trying to find some nonexistent cover, until finally I said, "What the hell" and just pulled my pants down and went quickly. The deel was going to be a lifesaver. At least, it would be if I could figure out how to ride in the thing.

It took a team to get us dressed and it took a team to get us on our ponies. The deels were bulky, like wearing thick quilts. One person held my horse while I climbed up. Then another person helped tuck in all the deel bits. I'm pretty sure I was a couple inches higher in the saddle as a result. Haven's response when he landed in his saddle was an immediate, "Nope." He climbed down and removed his deel. "It's going to be hard enough learning to ride in this saddle without also fighting with my clothing," he said.

Carly didn't even try. She had her deel off and packed safely away.

Brandon and I kept ours on. I didn't know what Brandon was thinking, but I was thinking things like *cultural immersion, comfort,* and *it was too hard getting up here, and I don't want to have to figure out how to get off right now.*

That lasted all the way to first break. The cold morning quickly transformed into a hot day, and I could not wait to peel that thing off and stow it away. It was good to know it was available, but so nice to be free of the burden.

Carly and Brandon were both riding the English/Western mash up saddle. Julie had her own custom Mongolian saddle. And they had brought another Mongolian saddle for Haven.

The Mongolian saddles were beautiful. They came in bright colors of red and orange, with large silver decorations on the seat and intricate embroidery and leather tooling down the fenders (the wide leather straps that connect the saddle to the stirrups and protect the rider's legs from rubbing against the horse). The craftsmanship was remarkable.

They also looked extremely painful. They were made from birch wood covered with a thin fabric. Their unforgiving *u* shape, formed by a high pommel (the front rise of the saddle) and cantle (the back rise), forced the rider to sit high above the horse. Imagine sitting in a rigid wooden cradle raised several inches above the horse's back, the pommel rising in front of you like a handle, the cantle behind you like a backrest, both working to keep you securely in place despite also making you feel precariously positioned above your horse. We were told that they are very comfortable once you got used to them. The "once you got used to them" part was where I checked out.

Haven, as a fundraising effort, promised his friends and family that he would ride the entire 700K in a Mongolian saddle, if they agreed to send money. It seemed he had a couple uncles who want to see him suffer, so the ploy worked fundraising-wise. We documented his climb and initial feelings about the saddle. "So far, so good," he said, not wanting to commit to anything beyond that just yet.

There was one really fancy Mongolian saddle on display off to the side. It wasn't getting put on a horse just yet, but we had all spent time covertly checking it out. At some point over the next few days, we would each need to ride at least 20K in it. After bearing each rider across the steppe, this magnificent saddle would find its new home at the Gala auction. I was thankful I wouldn't have to deal with that on Day One.

I overheard part of a conversation between Carly and Haven.

"I only have the clothes I have," said Carly.

"Deep thoughts by Carly," joked Haven.

And I thought her words were indeed profound. There was a stark truth in her simple statement. We come to our challenges with what we have—nothing more and nothing less. No wishing was going to give me stronger legs or a tougher spirit. No amount of regret would bring back the months of training I could have done. My strength, my fears, my grief, my determination—these were what I had to work with. Like Carly's limited wardrobe, I would have to make it be enough.

I named my horse on Day One—Sparky—because he reminded me of a Fourth of July sparkler, a small but intense light. Sparky was as happy as I was to be heading out.

Sparky didn't like it when I patted him, and Julie explained the Mongolian horses weren't treated the same way as they were in America. They were a lot more hands off. And I giggled to myself, wondering what she would think of my unconventional approach to bonding with Roan. During those dark winter evenings after work, when riding wasn't possible, I'd pull up a camp chair in his stall and read aloud. Charlie thought I was slightly crazy, but he'd join us anyway, setting up his own chair in the corner. While I read and Roan munched his hay, Charlie would carve little wooden birds, his knife making soft scratching sounds between my words.

The three of us created our own strange little routine: horse, wife, and husband, each doing our own thing but somehow together.

The memory made me smile, and I forgave Sparky for not wanting to be petted. It wasn't his fault no one read to him as a child.

Learning to Ride Mongolian Style

We had camped near the Wild Kerlin River, which, unlike its name, had a gentle, winding flow. It was an ancient river that showed its age by its twists and turns as it meandered through grassland that was turning golden brown in the face of fall's cooling temperatures.

My height, though increased by the size of my pony, felt insignificant. Mongolian ponies are, on average, 12–14 hands tall. A "hand" is the standard measurement for horse height. This comes from a time when it was easiest to measure something using an actual body part, and a hand is easier to hold against a horse than, for example, a foot. For consistency, a hand equals four inches, so Mongolian ponies are, on average, 48–56 inches at the withers. The withers are the highest point on the horse's back, located at the base of the neck between the shoulder blades. Therefore, when I say my height was increased by the height of my pony, you know we aren't talking a significant gain. Combined, we would be small in almost any landscape. But in that one, we were miniscule.

I looked back at our camp. A few minutes ago, it had been my entire world. My home away from home. And now I could see how insignificantly small it was surrounded by all that land and not one other shelter in sight.

I know I keep saying how small I felt, and how big the land felt, and you might be thinking, *OK, lady, I got it*, but I don't think you do. Because it was more than the physical. It was suddenly realizing just how far away I was from everything I knew. It was suddenly realizing just how vulnerable I was in this big, wide world.

How my resources for survival all came down to a few items and a handful of strangers. And, even scarier, I was suddenly feeling the full impact of how my decisions every day prior led me to this moment. And, suddenly worried, I was not up for this. Panic bubbled in my stomach. But then Charlie's voice, once again, "Sometimes the only way out is through it."

Deep breath.

Face forward.

Ride.

We moved across the landscape like a scene from an old Western movie. Baagii, at point, was reading the land with eyes trained from a lifetime of experience. Lhaagva brought up the rear, his watchful presence keeping us together; Julie wove between the front and back like a thread binding me, my three teammates, and Ashley as we all clustered in the middle; Tom and Bayaraa followed in the van; and a young guide herded our spare horses.

The earth stretched before us like the washboard stomach of some giant beast, well-defined muscles beneath a layer of golden-brown skin. I imagined in the spring, it was covered in lush, green grasses, swaying in spring winds, inviting livestock to eat and be fat. But it was fall now, and this section had been grazed down to short nubs, which highlighted one of the challenges of this ride: A straight line to the finish might be nice, but, instead, we would zigzag in constant search of food for our horses. Our route would stick to the river valley as much as possible for this very reason. Today's destination was somewhere beyond the curve of the earth.

We were on our way. I decided to be cautiously optimistic. Today was about making sure our saddles were adjusted correctly, a process more complex than I initially realized. From my familiar world of Western riding, I understood basic saddle adjustment—getting the stirrup length right, making sure the saddle sits level. But here, watching the guides work with the other riders on their Russian Army surplus saddles, I sensed they were checking different things. Through gestures and translated fragments of conversation, they seemed to be evaluating not just stirrup length, but also how each rider's weight balanced on their mount.

I watched Lhaagva and another rider watch me. Their heads nodded to different points while they conversed in their soft language. And then Lhaagva rode over and told me what to do. There was a fraction of a second when I felt defensive, but I stomped that thing right out. Now was not the time to be cocky. I was a student here, learning from a man whose knowledge of horses runs as deep as the steppes themselves, passed down through generations who lived and died by their horsemanship. He knew horsemanship like the ocean knows salt. Of course, he had things to teach me.

I never had formal riding lessons. The closest I came to it was when Bud, my stepdad, pointed me to a horse and told me what he wanted the horse to do. For example, to train a horse to make tight turns, he had me race them as fast as possible along the fence, and then, last minute, turn them sharply into the fence and race back the other way. In order to develop the muscle that allowed a horse to explode out of the roping box, he had me race them up the steepest hills we could find, leaning forward, urging them faster. He had me practice sharp stops and then leaning into it and backing up. I learned to unlatch, pass through, and re-latch gates without dismounting. I was taught to ride in any length of stirrup because I was often warming the horse up for another rider. While I enjoyed trail riding, it was without knowledge of how specifically to hold my reins or maintain a gait for hours on end.

But Lhaagva was a good teacher. We didn't speak the same language, but he could mime effectively, and I could ask a question with an eyebrow raise and a gesture. He fixed my hand position and my reins. He nodded when I got it right. If he needed to tell me more, he rode away, and a few minutes later, Julie would ride up and say, "Lhaagva says..." And so began my intensive Mongolian horseback riding lessons.

In Mongolia, horsemanship flows from understanding the herd. Lhaagva taught through his whole body—a slight shift in his seat, a gentle motion of his hands, a quiet clicking sound and a louder "Choo Choo," which is the Mongolian equivalent of "Giddy up!" He rode up beside me and reached over to adjust my grip on the reins, his weathered hands positioning mine with the precision of a craftsman. He showed me with a light touch how to let the horse find its rhythm within the group. He found a stick for me, which he encouraged me to use as I would a crop back home, with a light hand, and only as a reminder that I'm here and I have an opinion about how fast we should go.

When he wanted to correct my posture, he demonstrated first, exaggerating the difference between what I was doing and what he wanted. His horse moved beneath him like water flowing over stones: effortless, natural. Then he watched as I tried to mirror him, nodding slightly and giving me his beautiful smile when I got closer to the mark. There was an efficiency to his teaching that made words unnecessary.

When we stopped for breaks, the guides dismounted first, and then they insisted we wait until one of them could take our horse's head and hold it while we dismounted. I suspect they have had too many ponies successfully make a break for it, causing chaos with the whole herd, to risk letting the foreign riders attempt this on our own. The guides moved through their tasks with practiced co-ordination, each knowing their role without discussion. I watched and tried to read the system, aware that I was somewhere between student and liability.

My most challenging lesson was that I was holding the reins wrong—too tense and uneven. Essentially, my emotions made manifest.

Brandon and Carly were receiving similar attention, but only Carly looked at me, and we smiled at each other.

It turned out that my previous experience wasn't entirely useless. There are some universal things: Keep your feet under you—if a horse trips, keep his head up, and that will help him regain his feet. Don't let hours of riding cause you to be lazy—you must stay sharp throughout.

And then I smiled to myself and to Charlie, who was invisible but riding beside me nevertheless. I may have been the worst rider out here, but I was out there. I was riding a horse in Mongolia!

Later, Julie rode up to both Carly and me. "Lhaagva says you both are doing really well. He appreciates how responsive you both are to his suggestions." And that was incredible to hear!

If only that lady who told me I was going to get bucked off could see me now!

The Rhythm

In interviews with athletes who take part in endurance events, someone always asks, "What do you think about during all those miles?"

I think this is a really important question. Because when you are in an event like this, what you think about determines your entire experience. On Day One, I thought happy thoughts. Things like, *I'm doing it!* and *This is actually happening!* and *Holy cow, that was amazing* after a solid thirty-minute (or more) canter.

But another thought I had on Day One was much more mundane and had to do with technique—specifically, posting. Posting is a riding technique that involves rising and falling in time with the horse's trot. It is supposed to make the ride more comfortable for both the horse and the rider, especially for long distance, by alleviating jarring from the impact of the sitting trot.

I was taught to post by using a two-count beat. Posting isn't a skill I use often in my trail riding back home. I live on the edge of the Cascade Mountains. Trail riding for me consists of steep inclines and treacherous declines, narrow trails of sandstone, fallen logs, and streams.

So, while I knew how to do it, slipping into counting mode helped me stay focused. Sometimes "one, two, one, two," sometimes, "one, two, three, four," and sometimes, "one and two and three and four and."

I even joked to myself about how each trot had its own count, its own personality, demanding different responses from both mind and body: the gentle trot, the "things are getting serious" trot, and the soul-crushing trot.

In the gentle trot, the rhythm of posting became a full-body meditation: up-down, rise-fall, following the horse's motion through my core and legs. It flowed naturally, my thighs lifting me just enough to float above the saddle before settling back down. The counting came as softly as breathing—"one-two, one-two"—matching the steady drum of hoofbeats on packed earth.

But as the pace quickened into the "things are getting serious" trot, every muscle engaged differently. My shoulders tightened, quads burning as they lifted me higher to match the increased momentum. The counting grew more urgent—"ONE-two-THREE-four"—helping me stay ahead of the jarring impact. The horizon bounced in my vision unless I focused on a distant point, letting my body absorb the motion while my mind clung to the rhythm.

The soul-crushing trot was pure survival mode. It turned my legs to concrete and my spine to glass. Just below a canter, it demanded perfect timing or risked throwing me completely offbeat. My counting turned into desperate prayer, each number gasped between impacts, muscles trembling with effort. The repetitive motion both exhausted and hypnotized. Like grief, it came in waves: moments of finding the rhythm followed by stretches of just holding on.

I hoped that, soon, I would not need to use counting as a crutch.

Later in the ride, I realized I already didn't need to count in order to post correctly, but the counting continued, regardless. Almost like a compulsion. The numbers ran consistently. I thought it would be nice if I could come up with some sort of motto that I could think of. I mean, if my thoughts were in a relentless loop, maybe they could at least be productive and convince my subconscious of something positive. But it was incredibly difficult to come up with a four-count motto. Plus, I was tired, which always affects my thinking.

For a while, my subconscious supplied, *You are worthy.*

I am worthy? Worthy of what? I didn't know. What a strange thing to think. It was an incomplete thought. I tried it anyway, but I simply couldn't accept the statement as is. So I rejected it.

Before I knew it, I was back to counting.

One, two, three, four
One, two, three, four

On about Day Three, I decided I did not always have to post. I practiced riding the trot, which broke up the routine. But even so, my brain held onto the counting.

Soon after I was back home and safe in my living room, I attempted to watch one video I had taken on my GoPro. I heard the horse's footfalls, and that relentless counting started right up in my mind. I had to turn off the video and do some deep breathing!

I did think of one motto of sorts to say that stuck with me longer than all the rest. It was four syllables: Ya, Ho, Va, Way.

Several years ago, I watched some YouTube video of a guy talking about each breath being a tiny prayer. And that, in fact, according to the video, the earliest name of God was a series of sounds made while breathing: "Ya" and "Va" on the in-breath, "Ho" and "Way" on the out-breath.

The counting became my heartbeat across the steppe, a

metronome marking time as we crossed this ancient land. When I finally found Ya, Ho, Va, Way, it felt like discovering a deeper rhythm beneath the surface count. "Ya" on the rise, "Ho" on the settle, "Va" lifting again, "Way" coming home to the saddle. Prayer and motion merged into one continuous flow, each breath a tiny connection to something larger than my aching body or worried mind. Out there, where the sky swallowed all sound except hoofbeats and wind, even counting became a form of meditation. Ya, Ho, Va, Way. I was doing the hardest thing I'd ever done physically, and I wanted my God with me every breath of the way.

Accidental Cow Herders

And so I rode and counted and chanted, but I watched the other riders, too. The late-morning sun cast short shadows that mirrored our choppy pace as we spread out in loose formation. Carly rode very straight, trying to find her rhythm and position in the strange saddle. Haven looked like a natural—relaxed and comfortable, his horse matching the easy sway of his body. Brandon looked like he was trying to recall all his lessons, his posture shifting between tense and deliberately relaxed. Ashley simply rode.

Up ahead, the grassland dipped into a shallow bowl where a herd of maybe thirty cows grazed—brown-and-black bodies dotting the landscape. Our path took us through the center of their gathering. The steady rhythm of our horses' hooves drew their attention, heads rising in unison as we approached, their mouths pausing mid-munch. They watched us warily, mooing the question, "Are you here to chase us?"

When we didn't answer, they talked about it amongst themselves.

"I think they're here to chase us."

"No, I think we're fine."

"No, really, I think we aren't supposed to be here!"

"Really? What do you think?"

"I think we should be moving."

And so the cows stopped grazing and ran before us in continued mooed conversation.

"How far do you think we need to go?"

"Are we supposed to go over here? Or over there?"

Haven and I looked at each other. "Are we herding cows now?" he asked.

I replied, "I think we are!"

And then one cow stopped and watched us pass. She mooed to the rest, "Hey, guys? I don't think they are chasing us. I think they are just passing through."

The other cows looked back and sort of wandered to a stop.

"Well, that was embarrassing!" they lamented.

Brandon Is Reborn

One of the first lessons Julie taught us was to look for gopher holes. They were hidden under built-up patches of dirt, and they were everywhere. You could recognize a tunnel system from a distance, but you had to be watching. Gopher warrens sprawl like a barely visible labyrinth, its slightly raised tunnels a camouflaged menace. The ground above seems firm until you learn to spot the loose earth and soft patches. For a rider on horseback, this false stability can betray with brutal swiftness. A single step on the fragile crust, and the earth caves in, swallowing the hoof, potentially wrenching the leg, sending horse and rider crashing down.

We rode single file and parallel to a weathered dirt road, keeping to the softer ground alongside. Occasional rocks dotted the terrain, not densely packed but enough to watch for. The gopher warrens were harder to spot, their loose dirt mounds disrupting the grass coverage like moth-eaten holes in a blanket. Some were obvious with fresh dirt piles, but others were treacherously concealed under thin grass, betrayed only by subtle dips in the ground's surface.

Julie told us this, and immediately Brandon rode straight through a gopher tunnel maze. His horse did not trip, but I was holding my breath. Julie repeated her instructions, but Brandon continued on merrily. And then we realized he had his headphones in. He couldn't hear.

Julie got close enough to him so that he finally pulled out his ear buds. She explained again about the gopher patches. Brandon still didn't seem to understand. I watched him squint at the ground, his gaze darting between terrain features, clearly trying to translate Julie's warnings into actionable guidance.

Brandon was new to horses—as I have already explained. One of the things he did to prepare was interview riders who had come to Mongolia. He shared some of the things he learned on our van ride out at the start of the ride.

"They say that you can just forget everything you've ever learned about riding. It is all different out there. The horses are different. The equipment is different." Those words had both scared and comforted me. At least I wasn't going to be the only one who was out of their element.

The afternoon of Day One, I was riding behind Brandon so that I could keep an eye on him. But I was feeling both the effort of riding and the monotony. The morning coolness had given way to an afternoon of heat. All of us had removed layers. I was down to a t-shirt. Haven was wearing a white button-down shirt. White? It seemed a bold choice given the heat and the dirt. Carly was in a black, sleeveless athletic top. And Brandon sported a blue tank-top.

I'd mostly given up worrying about Brandon's horse-tripping. I wasn't sure how he had made it this far. I decided he had a magic horse.

He didn't.

The moment his horse went down is seared in my memory like a slow-motion video. His horse's head dropped suddenly as its legs crumpled underneath. Brandon's body pitched forward, his arms wind milling for balance. The reins slipped through his fingers as his horse's shoulder dipped sharply left. Brandon was launched from the saddle like a stone from a sling, his bare shoulder leading his trajectory.

His body rotated midair, dust pluming around him as he hit the ground. The impact drove a sharp "oof" from his lungs. He rolled once, twice, stirring up small clouds, before coming to rest on his butt, legs splayed out in front of him. His GoPro hung crooked from his helmet, still faithfully recording.

The horse scrambled up and bolted, stirrups flapping empty against its sides. It passed through our spread-out line—first Carly, about thirty feet ahead, who glanced at it without really seeing it; then Haven, another twenty feet up, who sat back in surprise; and then past Baagii at the front. Even from fifty yards ahead, I could see Baagii's eyes widen in surprise as he looked back over his shoulder. His surprise shifted to a knowing half-smile, the look of someone who's seen this scene play out a hundred times before. Then he turned his horse to chase and reclaim Brandon's mount.

While the crew sprang into action around me—Julie shouting to the medical van, Lhaagva racing after Baagii—I remained frozen, holding my breath. Through my own suspended moment of worry, I watched Brandon's face for signs of how bad this was. His eyes were wide with surprise, dust coating one side of his face and shoulder. The red mark on his shoulder was already promising an impressive bruise.

I was watching him closely because how Brandon responded to this moment would set the tone for how we as a group would respond when things go wrong. In the suspended silence, a hundred scenarios flashed through my mind. Would he unleash frustration at the horse, at himself? Would his CEO composure crack under the weight of public failure? Or would this be the moment he decided this whole adventure was too much?

And beneath these questions lay a deeper current of worry. His shoulder was already reddening where it scraped the ground. The way he landed could have easily resulted in broken bones, or worse. If he was seriously injured on Day One, what did that mean for the rest of us?

The silence stretched while I watched him, dust settling around his still form. His shoulders tensed slightly, his jaw tightening—telltale signs of someone wrestling with embarrassment. Here he was, the accomplished CEO who spent months preparing, thrown from his horse on Day One. I could almost see the internal battle playing across his face, the instinct to prove himself warring with the reality of what just happened.

Brandon stood up slowly, his GoPro still hanging crooked and forgotten on his helmet. His bare shoulder scratched angry red, but his face showed a deliberate shift, choosing to meet our concerned gazes with a smile that, while shaky, was genuine. It was a small heroic act of courage, choosing humor over humiliation. I felt pride, even though I had nothing to do with any of it. Still, I was proud of Brandon.

Tom was scanning Brandon's body with the focused intensity of someone who's seen too many accidents go bad. Soon, he pronounced him good to ride.

Brandon remounted, shakily gathering his reins, with Baagii holding his horse's head. The saddle leather creaked as he settled his weight, his horse shifted restlessly beneath him. To give him a couple extra moments to compose himself, Julie told us that, in Mongolia, when you fall off your horse, the ground you land on is your new birthing place. You are born again here, and that little spot of dirt is now yours. And so we called Brandon a Mongolian landowner, which seemed to please him.

Brandon paid more attention to gopher holes after that. His eyes now scanned the terrain ahead with new respect, though his earbuds were still pumping music as he was mentally crafting how this story would play on social media. His "rebirth" on Mongolian soil didn't completely transform him, but it taught him something vital: The steppe demands attention, whether you are ready to give it or not.

How Many Kids Do You Have?

At the end of the first day, I was feeling encouraged. I knew it was a half-day, but I thought I might actually be able to do this. We arrived at camp with plenty of daylight left, and I collapsed into one of the camp chairs, its metal frame creaking under my weight, the canvas seat still warm from the afternoon sun. Around us, the camp buzzed with end-of-day activity. The cook and Tuya moved around their portable stoves, the rhythmic thunk-thunk-thunk of vegetables being chopped mixing with the metallic clink of pots and the soft whoosh of propane burners. Steam carried the rich scent of something savory cooking—lamb, maybe? The crew worked with practiced efficiency to set up our tents, the snap and rustle of canvas mixing with their quiet conversations in Mongolian.

We had said goodbye to Ashley. He and his camera went home with a promise to see us at the finish line! "You will be different then," he vowed.

"Changed?" I asked.

"Less clean," he said with a chuckle. "A lot less clean."

Haven, Brandon, Carly, and I sat around a fold-up table. Someone had set out water and nuts. The familiar ritual of sharing food and drink felt almost surreal after hours in the saddle. We were waiting while our tents were set up and an official meal was prepared. I felt a little spoiled, and like I should do something. But then I thought, *Naw. I'm just going to sit here.* I was pleasantly tired. Sore, but not dying.

I watched the crew untack each mount (which means they removed their tack to include saddles and bridles) and then check the horses over before fitting hobbles (simple rope restraints that look almost primitive to my Western-trained eyes). Unlike the stables from home, with their solid fences and locked gates, horses here were kept close through an ancient practice that seemed to respect their partial freedom. The crew looped the ropes around three legs—I thought it was both front legs and one back, leaving one leg free for defense, though in the gathering darkness I never got a clear-enough look to be certain. The setup left just enough slack for the horses to graze and move at a walk—even defend themselves, if needed—but prevented them from a faster pace that would let them stray too far.

The horses accepted this nighttime ritual with the same pragmatic attitude they showed toward everything else. They continued grazing while the crew worked, then spread out in loose groups across the landscape, their shapes growing indistinct in the gathering darkness. Someone from the crew would check on them periodically through the night, a responsibility I didn't fully appreciate until later.

When we arrived at base camp last night, we were given bins for our personal items. Bins were easier to haul from camp to camp than luggage. They stacked nicer, and we could use them as extra seating. Everything I didn't need to haul around the country stayed in my luggage and went back with the driver to Ulaanbaatar. My gala dress, for example.

Can we talk about my gala dress for a second?

The Gala was part two of the fundraising we would do as riders of the Gobi Gallop. Part one was our entry fee. Part two was a huge formal event at the end of the ride that was attended by dignitaries and businessmen of Mongolia and ambassadors from the different embassies in Ulaanbaatar.

I had never been to a Gala event of any size, let alone one with ambassadors and dignitaries. I needed just the right outfit. It needed to be elegant. It would need to look good, even if I had ridiculous tan lines after all this. It was going to have to survive three weeks in my luggage and still not need pressing. And then, you know, the big question: How much cleavage was appropriate to show when in a foreign country at an event like this? Should it be dignified? Should it be sexy? And also, what kind of shoes? I had purchased a black dress, which I was looking forward to wearing. The off-the-shoulder sleeves made my boobs look fantastic. But a few months before the Gobi Gallop, they were wrapping up the Blue-Wolf totem, and they posted pictures of their gala attire, and they all looked like diplomats. I showed my friend Jill my dress, and then the Blue-Wolf Totem picture and she said, "You have a dress problem."

So there I was, dress shopping again. I finally went with a deep-blue conservative-yet-elegant floor-length dress with silver edging. My daughters each gave it a thumbs up for the right blend of sexy/diplomatic.

Anyway, that dress and the matching shoes went back to Ulaanbaatar with my luggage. Unfortunately, so did my hair-brush. I didn't know how I missed it.

"Well, I guess I don't have to brush my hair this entire outing," I said out loud. And Carly came to my rescue: "You can use my brush!" she said, and she ran and got it.

I took out a braid and started brushing one-half of my head. Then I re-braided that side and took out the other side for brushing. My scalp tingled pleasantly under the bristles, each stroke releasing the day's tension along with tangles. The simple act of caring for myself, of restoring order to one small thing I could control, felt unexpectedly fantastic. The late-afternoon light softened to honey-gold, casting long shadows across our little circle while we shared handfuls of nuts and talk. As I worked the brush through my hair, the conversation drifted to homes and family left behind. The question on the floor was, do you have kids? If so, how many, and what are their ages?

Carly reported she didn't have children.

Brandon said he had two, and I was surprised by this news, though I didn't know why. He said they were ages six and ten.

Haven said he had one son, age fifteen.

And I said I had three daughters, ages twenty-seven, twenty-three, and twenty-two. I gave birth to two. The third was the daughter of my late husband.

I said "late husband" casually, as if the words didn't cause my heart to ache. As if it was no big deal.

But slight movements from my team revealed they understood.

Carly's hand lowered to her chest. Haven's eyes softened in recognition and understanding that loss isn't just about the past but also about all the futures that will never happen. Brandon was the first to voice his feelings. "I'm so sorry," he said in that gentle tone people use when they get it.

I was so thankful to be brushing my hair. Thankful I had a reason not to make eye contact. But also incredibly grateful to Brandon that he didn't let it slide by.

And so I told my team about my Charlie.

Obituary
Printed in the *Wenatchee World*, September 2021

Charles David "Charlie" Lundin
June 26, 1972–August 29, 2021
Wenatchee, Washington

The next time you are sorting firewood, stop and remember Charles (Charlie) Lundin who passed away at the age of 49 from injuries related to a severe stroke in Harborview Medical Center, Seattle, WA on Sunday August 29th. We were blessed to learn so many valuable lessons from Charlie, one of which was to always sort your firewood according to what burns the hottest, what smells the best, and what will taste the best when used to cook.

Also: always check the path behind you when you are hiking, so that it looks familiar when you are on your way out.

Keep way more food on hand than you can ever eat. Hide it in unpredictable places (in the closet, under the bed, under the bench in your garage.) Don't tell anyone about it. Hand it out generously when someone you know is in need.

Don't let things like being told you will never walk again stop you. On your way to learning to walk again, start building your own cabin. Slow progress is still progress.

Turn down an invitation from Oprah to speak about your time trapped under a house for 30 hours and the subsequent recovery because you don't like to travel.

Still be willing to travel to Africa with your wife, simply because she wants you there.

When you have been thinking about someone all day, call them or send a text. They might need you. Don't bother about grammar or spelling, they can sound it out.

Wake your children with weird random duck calls. Hand them money on the sly and then complain loudly that "These kids are taking all my money!"

Give up the habits that hold you back. Choose to be a father over alcohol. Keep making that choice every day for 21 years.

Move into a new neighborhood. Meet your neighbors. Introduce your neighbors who have been living there for years, to each other, for the first time.

Know that not every silence has to be filled.

Know that the best way to manage chronic pain is by focusing on others. There is incredible strength and selflessness in being kind to people when you are hurting.

Above all, talk to the Big Guy daily. Feel sorry for those who don't know him yet because life is so much better with God. Share the word of God through actions and leave the preaching to others.

On Day One, we traveled 47K, or 30 miles.

5
Day Two

Humility

Date: September 12, 2022
Distance: 69K, or 43 miles

On Day Two, I woke up and thought, *I should get some pictures.* I fished through my bin for my camera. Brandon and Carly were speaking quietly outside and laughing. I crawled out of my tent to see them walking toward the river. They were shrouded in the morning mist that was rising from the river and meeting the valley fog that drifted over the land. I snapped a picture. Then I turned around...and caught my breath.

The horses!

Fog clung to the valley in delicate wisps, curling and shifting like a living thing. It wrapped itself around the horses, trailing along their legs and rising to brush their flanks, softening their outlines until they looked more like creatures from legend than pasture. The mist caught the morning light, refracting it into a gentle glow that crowned their heads and backs with halos of gold. They moved slowly, their forms half-revealed, as if stepping between worlds, their breath steaming in the cool air like whispers of some ancient, forgotten magic.

I snapped pictures all the way to the temporary outhouse the crew had set up. The outhouse was more concept than construction, a hopeful hole in the ground with three canvas walls that did little more than suggest privacy. The fourth side was wide open, so I enjoyed a beautiful view while I did my business. To use the facilities, we had to squat with one foot on either side of the hole and try our best to not hit our pants or boots. Peeing outside is not a talent that comes easy to me. When I was a kid and we were out in the pasture, having way too much fun to run all the way inside, I tried, but my results were less than ideal. I sort of developed a fear of the job and avoided it whenever possible. But it was on the trip I took with Charlie to Africa, while we were out on safari, that I finally mastered the skill. When you are with a group of women, all peeing at once, while the men stand in a circle with their backs to you, facing out watching for lions, you learn a few things. The key is to squat low and balance your weight on the balls of your feet.

Once that was done, I noticed Haven starting his Tai Chi. I quickly put away my camera and joined him.

Practicing Tai Chi while the sun rises over the Mongolian Steppe might just be the coolest thing I will ever do in my entire life. My foot hooked the ground. Not a step, but a deliberate root—toes first, then heel, weight shifting like water finding its level. Haven's hand was a whisper at my elbow, guiding without touching.

"Yang foot," he said. The frost crackled beneath me. Each blade of grass was a crystal, catching the first light like a thousand tiny prisms. My breath formed clouds that merged with the morning mist hovering just inches above the ground. My left hand moved first—not a wave, but a slow unfurling. Fingers curled, then spread slightly, like a leaf opening, like a wing testing the first breath of morning. My right hand followed, a mirror image. Symmetry. Balance.

Haven breathed. I heard it. A rhythm older than words.

The steppe stretched. No trees. No buildings. Just grass, the color of honey and wheat meeting the black-blue of a predawn sky. And us. Two silhouettes moving so slowly we might be part of the landscape.

My shoulders, tight from travel and worry, began to soften. Not relaxing. Releasing. There was a difference. Like a locked gate slowly giving way—not because someone was breaking through, but because it chose to open. A crane called in the distance. A single, pure note that hung in the air like a question.

I am here, my body answered. *I am still here.*

The morning air bit with unexpected sharpness, a reminder that it was autumn. It carried the faint earthy scent of dew-kissed grass. As the sun continued to rise, its light pierced the fog in shafts of molten gold, illuminating the world in ethereal brilliance.

We completed the last bow, and immediately the sounds of camp crashed over me. People in motion, gathering, packing, cooking.

Breakfast was called, and we ate. There were eggs and some sort of sausage-type meat. I also grabbed some granola. Coffee was next and then getting my water ready for the day.

Tom and Julie handed out ibuprofen, and I took some. Tai Chi had loosened me up, but my knees were feeling the strain from yesterday's ride, and today we would be riding twice as far.

Now it was time to really get moving. I tried to figure out my layering. It was chilly, but I wasn't sure what the day would bring, so I went with a t-shirt under a fleece coat. I put my riding gloves in my back pocket, then I packed up my sleeping bag and all the things that would go in the truck. And then packed a separate bag, which I would have access to at lunch. I put things in there like rain gear, extra gloves, painkiller, my granola, and my camera. Already, I was developing a routine. Now I went to wait for the horses.

When we mounted up and Haven's rear end touched the saddle, he said, "Oh, there I am!"

And I could relate when I followed. The aches and pains from day one were all present and accounted for.

• • •

When I mounted my horse, I immediately knew his name was Brandy. He barely noticed me. He was too distracted by tiny flies that were pestering him. He was waving his head up and down, up and down. Even after we began to ride, his head was in relentless motion, and I had no idea how he could do that and still walk and trot in a straight line. I tried this later on my own at home, nodding my head and walking. I almost fell down.

Brandy's head movements only slowed when we were at the canter. Otherwise, I felt like he was drunk; thus, his name must be either Rum or Brandy. Brandy was what stuck because in my mind, Brandy is a beautiful brown color. Later, I found out it is actually red. Obviously, I don't know my alcohol. Whatever. I was pretty sure Brandy did not care.

When we rode out, I sang "Brandy (You're a Fine Girl)," a song that was number one on the Billboard Hot 100 chart in August 1972, the year I was born.

I was not the only one to name my horse. All of us riders did it. It was our way of showing affection and attempting connection. But, traditionally, Mongolian horses aren't named, for reasons ranging from the sacred to the practical—naming implies ownership, which contrasts with the respectful bond Mongolians share with their animals, and practical descriptors like 'white stallion' serve better in a nomadic lifestyle where herds are large and constantly moving.

Haven's was the only horse whose name came with him. He was named by Julie: Reprobate. We learned that Reprobate was a Gobi Gallop veteran. He had carried riders for eight of the nine years that the gallop had been in existence. He arrived with his brother, and the two of them were inseparable. Reprobate insisted on always trotting alongside his brother. This got to be a problem when the riders had different ideas, which is how he earned his name.

I liked the look of Reprobate. His dark gray coat and long black mane that fell over his eyes gave him the look of a brooding teenager at a punk concert—too cool to care about anything, including the rider on his back. But Haven connected to him right away and renamed him Kevin Smith, a filmmaker/actor/writer often associated with dark humor and countercultural themes.

Julie told us on Day One, "This is not the time to suffer silently. If you need your gear adjusted in any way, then we will do it."

Still, it went against my nature to make the entire party stop just so I could adjust my stirrups. I tried my best to get the length right before we headed out. Yesterday, my right leg was hurting pretty badly. Today, I decided to try a shorter length. After the morning, my left leg started hurting. So I tried lengthening the left one, keeping the right one short. Turns out, that was a terrible idea. So then I just decided my legs were going to have to take turns hurting.

Lhaagva was our guide for Day Two. Baagii had gone back to look for more horses. Lhaagva set a pace of trot, walk, trot, walk, which was delightful.

For non-riders, the difference between gaits is a bit like shifting gears in a car. Walking is first gear—steady, slow, and comfortable. Trotting is second gear—a two-beat rhythm wherein diagonal pairs of legs move together, creating that distinctive bouncing motion that requires riders to either post (rise and fall with the movement) or sit deep to absorb the impact. Cantering is third gear—a smooth, three-beat rolling motion that feels like flying when done right. Galloping is full throttle—a four-beat rhythm in which all hooves leave the ground for a moment. Lhaagva's pattern of alternating between walk and trot was like a long-distance runner finding their sustainable pace.

When I said Baagii had gone to look for more horses, I meant that he had lost a few. Horses here were allowed to free-range graze when they weren't needed for work. Then, when they were needed, their owner would ride out and gather them up. Baagii had spent the week before the ride doing just that, gathering them up. But he hadn't found them all. So we were a few horses short. When Baagii received word that his horses were spotted in a certain valley, he went to retrieve them. It was important that we have enough horses for us to switch out on a consistent basis so that we didn't overwork any of them.

The logistics of horse management were precise: For our seven riders, they'd brought eleven horses total. This ratio of roughly one-and-a-half horses per rider meant each horse could have a rest day every third day, crucial for maintaining their stamina over such long distances. Having enough horses, and keeping track of them, wasn't just about convenience; it was essential for the well-being of the animals carrying us across the steppe.

This whole process confused me. I knew that we spent a full day in a van riding to our starting point. I imagined that to retrieve his horses, Baagii was making that same drive back to his home base, then he would spend hours riding to that particular valley, gathering the horses, getting them loaded into a truck, and then back out to find us on the trail. Who knew when we would see him again?

The day started cool, but by lunch it was so hot, I wanted to put on my tank top. But I hadn't packed it in my day bag. "You have a sports bra on, right?" Carly asked. "Just wear that!"

I looked around at everyone. "Do you think that's OK? I mean, are there cultural things I should be aware of?"

Julie said, "It's OK. They know you are not Mongolian. They expect you to do things differently."

We had learned that a woman wearing a deel, if she had the top two buttons undone, was considered a hussy. Or, at least, she was sending out an invitation. The top two buttons on a deel, whether done or undone, offer absolutely no difference in the amount of skin visible. So I felt like riding in just a sports bra was risky. Though Tom did nod approvingly and say, "That's a good look for you." I took the compliment for what it was and didn't read anything into it.

I felt like a warrior reborn, fierce and unyielding, riding across the vast steppes. The sun kissed my bare shoulders, my French braids skimmed the nape of my neck like the brief brush of a battle standard, my only armor a sports bra and the fire in my veins.

I was also bare-headed. I left my helmet at home because I had read in the paperwork that helmets were available. They suggested that if you have an unusually large or small head, bring your own helmet. I figured I had an average head, and after many hours of weighing and repacking, it got left behind.

"There is nothing average about you," Haven said when I explained to Julie why I didn't have a helmet. And I smiled at him. He didn't like hearing people talk badly about themselves.

The thing is, I forgot to mention to Julie that I didn't bring a helmet, and so no helmets were loaded into the vehicles. And so I was going to be riding 700K across Mongolia with no helmet.

But helmets were a new thing for me, anyway. Growing up with the rodeo crowd, we scoffed at helmets. Cowboys are invincible, it seems. I decided to embrace that concept. I already had "Don't fall off your horse," on my list, so I was covered.

Julie took a couple hours off from riding to follow us in the medic van and run the drone. Tom took a turn riding, using Julie's horse. Tom had very little horse-riding experience, and Julie rode a custom Mongolian saddle.

One kilometer in her Mongolian saddle, and he didn't look like he was having fun. He sat with one hand holding the reins, the other on the front of the Mongolian saddle. He was using the hand on the saddle to hold himself back in an effort to reduce the crushing of his groin. His face was furrowed in a scowl of concentration.

Carly had been watching him. Finally she said, "Let's change horses."

I was surprised and impressed by her offer. She said, "It's a lot to ask, not having ridden much at all, let alone now riding in a Mongolian saddle." So, instead, she generously hauled her sore self into this saddle.

I was still in awe, and I wondered, *Who is this woman I am riding across Mongolia with?* Empathetic to the point that she would increase her pain to reduce someone else's. In fact, I thought it physically hurt her to watch Tom's discomfort.

Riding by Myself

"You spend most of your life inside your head...make it a nice place to be."

—Meme posted by Women's Freedom Ride

Riding in Mongolia was a very solitary experience, no matter how big or small your team. The wind was a living force—not gusting but constantly pressing, stealing words from my mouth and thoughts from my mind, an endless rush that became the soundtrack of existence. It tugged at clothing and whipped loose strands of hair across my face. Conversation became impossible beyond shouted single words or hand signals. We spread out naturally, each in our own bubble of wind-noise and motion, together but isolated.

And that is life, too, isn't it? Each one of us is traveling through life with companions but still experiencing it in a way that is uniquely our own.

I have never truly been on my own. I am, and always have been, surrounded by love and family and friends. Many of them are suffering right alongside me with the loss of Charlie.

Even when riding close enough to see the sweat on Haven's neck or to catch Carly's grimace of discomfort, we might as well be miles apart. Like grief, you can be holding someone's hand, seeing their tears match yours, and still feel like you're the only person who's ever hurt this much. We were five riders moving as one unit across the steppe, each sealed in our private bubble of wind-noise and memories, together in our isolation.

Somewhere on Day Two, somewhere in the four-count beat of hooves against earth, my mind pulled up a memory. The rhythm became a metronome, pulling me back to another time when horses meant escape.

I was twelve years old. My mother was a single parent, and we had little money. On top of that, for a variety of reasons, we moved a lot. I changed schools every year. As a result, I was a lonely child, but my reading life was amazing.

And there were good people around me. Mic and BJ McCauley, for example, sold me Breezy, a nineteen-year-old quarter horse, for $150—and they took monthly payments of $10. I delivered newspapers for the *Wenatchee World* to pay for him and his board, my canvas bag heavy with rolled papers and black ink that stained the creases of my palms like tiny road maps.

Breezy and I explored every inch of the hills outside Omak, WA, his hooves kicking up dust that smelled like sage. While riding him, I moved between reality and imagination as easily as switching gaits. In my mind, we visited elephants and lions in Africa, practiced leaping into trees like Tarzan, and landing on his back like Zorro (with mixed, and mostly painful, results). We smuggled imaginary gold and explored unfamiliar territory. I was at that perfect age where fantasy and reality blend and become one. Everything was real and possible.

The day I had to sell Breezy remains in sharp focus. The broken sidewalk leading to the peeling paint of their house. The bleary-eyed man, tired from his night shift, the smell of cigarettes, a red-and-green crocheted afghan on the back of a chair. A little girl chattering away about her wonderful new horse while the man fished through his wallet for my $150.

I hated them all.

The door closed in front of me, and I stood there, $150 in my hand, watching it close on my childhood. I was selling Breezy because my mother was a single parent. And a newspaper route simply wasn't enough with all the expenses of a horse. And it was all too hard. I had made the difficult decision to sell him so my mother would have less to worry about. I was trading my horse for my mother.

And I would do it again.

I turned away from that door and made my first steps into adulthood. That perfect place between fantasy and reality slipped away.

I took in a sharp breath, looked around me with new eyes. My horse was moving beneath me; pure adventure was in front of me. Right here, right now, Mongolia felt like coming full circle. That space between fantasy and reality that I'd lost at twelve had opened again, but this time I was not just imagining adventures in faraway lands—I was living them. Each hoof beat carried me further from that girl standing on a broken sidewalk, further from that woman sitting in that hospital cafeteria, closer to someone who can still dream but also make those dreams real.

I wasn't just doing it. *I was becoming it.*

Have You Ever Written a Love Letter?

On the evening of Day Two, Carly asked, "Have you ever written a love letter?"

I was beginning to suspect that Carly had researched and gathered "icebreaker" questions in preparation for our evening conversations. She seemed to have several in the queue. I respected this! In fact, I had done that myself, but mine got left at home.

The answer for each of us was yes, we have. Seems to have been a high school thing, though I still write them. I write them more now than I ever have in my life. I had a journal in my luggage, in fact, where each entry started with "Dearest Charlie." I was writing to tell him about everything.

I think that when we lose people close to us, the "Halo Effect" can take over and we remember only the amazing things about that person. This was true for me and Charlie until one day, when I remembered that my Charlie was not perfect. I think this was an important step for me in my grieving. Everyone experiences grief differently. For me, there seemed to be a lot of guilt, a personal beating for all the ways I wasn't a great wife. But remembering that he was also flawed was helpful. And it just makes me marvel at the miracle of marriage. Two broken people committing to figuring it out together. Not a perfect union, but made more magical and precious because of it.

Memories of Charlie came in snapshots at this point—some sharp and clear, others soft around the edges like old photographs. One of my favorites was from the beginning.

"Mom, can we have dinner at Okie Charlie's?" This was my daughter, Nicole, age 4. Okie was how she pronounced "Uncle," and I could see Charlie cringe at the word. He didn't want my girls to think of him as their uncle. He had other plans. But he didn't correct her.

"Are you inviting us to dinner?" I asked him.

"I've got the crock pot on," he said, the smell of simmering beef stew drifting from his kitchen. "Can't eat it all myself."

Charlie and I had gone to the same high school, where he never spoke to me because, as he later claimed with a grin to anyone who would listen, "She was way out of my league."

A building had collapsed on him when he was twenty-one, crushing him so severely his foot touched his cheek. He survived thirty-six hours trapped in February mountain cold, and doctors said he'd never walk again. But when we met years later, he was not only walking; he had me and my girls dancing his made-up knee-slapping dance in his kitchen.

Charlie was the kind of neighbor who showed up with firewood before I knew I needed it, who cleaned my fireplace and fixed my washer. He called it "courting"; I thought he was just being kind. For some people, romance happens over candlelight and good food. Ours happened over chores and checklists.

We supported each other's interests from the start, even when those interests included crazy ideas, like riding horses in Mongolia.

I was tired and sore, but the smell of our dinner, served by Tuya, reminded me of Charlie's crock pot, savory aromas drifting from our bowls. It made me feel sentimental, like I was falling in love again. Tuya smiled at me and then asked Julie to translate for her. "Only the best people come to Mongolia to ride the Gobi Gallop. The bravest and the kindest. I'm so glad to meet all of you."

We rode 69K on Day Two, making our total distance so far 116K, or 72 miles.

6

Day Three

False Rock Bottom

Date: September 13, 2022
Distance: 70K, or 44 miles

"Good morning!" Julie said when she entered the breakfast tent. The place was buzzing. Plates of sausage, fried eggs, and potatoes landed on the table, and my team and the crew reached over and around one another to snatch up what they wanted. I looked at the food and felt my stomach vote for a hard pass. I grabbed my granola instead.

"You need protein," Haven said disapprovingly, but he wasn't speaking to me. Carly was also considering the food with hesitation. She gave me a side eye, and I quirked an eyebrow back.

"Not feeling good?" Brandon asked, to which Carly gave a non-committal shrug. "I have something for that!" he said and dashed out the door. He returned a few moments later with a medicine bag. If Tom was our official doctor, Brandon was our official pharmacist. I didn't know what was in that bag, though I admit I was curious.

"Do you have something for a bad attitude?" I asked, giving Tom the side eye.

Tom glared at me over the top of his coffee cup, and I grinned at him.

"I do!" Brandon said.

And I was surprised. "Really?"

"Yep, but you'll have to take this other pill to bring you back down later." Brandon rummaged through his collection of prescriptions and supplements with the enthusiasm of a tech CEO who'd found a way to optimize human performance through chemical enhancement.

Haven's expression was a study in diplomatic discomfort, his years of teaching Tai Chi and Eastern medicine visibly wrestling with his natural inclination to let others find their path. When Brandon held up a particularly colorful assortment of pills, Haven's carefully neutral face twitched.

"Oh, um, I'll pass for now," I said as I raised my first dose of ibuprofen to my lips.

"Fifteen minutes, everyone. Fifteen minutes!" Julie announced.

Tom grabbed his topped-off thermos in one hand and biscuit in the other and headed out. Brandon tossed everything back in his bag and also headed out. Haven started putting on his boots. Carly sighed and sat back. "They aren't going to leave without us," she said, clearly finding it difficult to be motivated.

Looking at Carly then reminded me of something I'd learned about endurance events. My research told me that on Day Three, the cumulative fatigue would be peaking. We would still be recovering from the first two days. The initial excitement would have worn off, leaving us in that mental gray zone where the finish line still felt impossibly far. Because our bodies won't have adapted to the demands yet, we would be in that brutal adjustment phase before finding our rhythm. I considered how I was feeling and decided that all this checked out. But if we could get through day three, then day four would be easier. We would adjust and we'd find our second wind.

I considered telling Carly all this and decided that she probably wasn't ready for a Pollyanna statement like "It's all gonna be better soon." So, I only gave her what I hoped was an encouraging smile and focused on my own preparations.

I had everything with me that I needed. My bags were already packed. Only one thing left, and that was to make up my waters for the day.

I had a secret I hadn't told anyone on the trip yet, and that was there were some foods I simply couldn't digest. Or, rather, I could digest them, it just took me more time and a lot more chewing. This was due to a stomach surgery I had done a few years ago. I didn't have special dietary considerations that would have needed to be disclosed when filling out the paperwork, but I did require more time to eat, and time was not something we had a lot of. So I did what I needed to do. I made a cocktail of nutrients that I could drink throughout the day. It wasn't a perfect solution. But it was a solution.

I knew today was going to be tough, but I was riding my personal wave of optimism that seemed to arrive with each sunrise. It was only a day. I could do anything for a day. And tomorrow would be better.

Looking back, I couldn't know then that hope was a morning thing, as predictable as sunrise and as vulnerable as mist. That it would start to evaporate with the first hours of riding, leaving me to navigate the afternoon with gritted teeth and stubborn will. But right then, in that crystalline moment, I believed I could do this.

I was back on Sparky, and I greeted him like an old friend. He did not share the sentiment. Still, he was willing. We started out with an easy walk, warming up to the day, with sweet Lhaagva in the lead. We trotted for a bit, then we walked, then we trotted. It was a nice pace. My aches and pains were working their way out. The morning air was crisp, reminding us that it was autumn. All seemed like it was going to be OK.

And then Baagii returned, and everything changed.

He came from behind at a mile eating fast trot. I watched him go by with trepidation and then glanced at Carly. She looked back, eyes wide and uncertain. She gave a little shrug. She didn't know what this meant either.

I didn't see any additional horses with him, which is what he had been away trying to gather. So his mission had been a fail? I suspected he was riding up to tell Lhaagva and Julie, and then we would all find out what was happening.

Instead, he galloped up to the front and kept right on going. Lhaagva immediately dropped to the side, indicating with a waving hand that we were supposed to follow Baagii. We all "Choo Choo!"'d to our ponies and attempted to keep up. Our ponies kicked up dust in their wake, and the steady clopping morphed into a frenetic beat. Baagii's pace was the soul-crushing trot just a beat slower than a canter.

After ten minutes, we were still doing that pace. After twenty minutes, we were still doing that pace. At thirty minutes, we were still doing that pace. Time lost all meaning, and we were still doing that pace.

Riding at that pace took concentration and strength. Legs needed to be held in, not flopping around. The rise and fall sequence tight, controlled, and precise. I've seen some riders in my life who look like they are almost gliding through the air, not moving. But that look of effortlessness is deceiving. It is only a sign of a good shock system—in this case, the rider's legs and back. And mine were working hard.

My eyes were focused forward scanning for gopher holes, and my mind was focused inward, counting desperately, when magic snuck up on me. My peripheral vision caught it first: a ripple of muscle, a flash of hide.

Horses!

Free and wild. Choosing to run with us.

Their muscles shifted beneath coats that changed with each stride—dappled grays bleeding into bronze, silver stuttering to deep chestnut. No uniform color, but a living canvas in motion. Square, earnest faces, looking forward. Lips in serious lines. Large, dark eyes reflecting the ground as it flickered past. Ears alert and twitching, listening and noticing.

With the soft chuff-chuff-chuff of hard breathing, each exhale punctuating their surge forward. The sounds were close and intimate. And louder, the drumbeat of hooves on bare earth, like the percussion section of a grand composition.

My chest tightened. Not pain. Something else. Recognition, maybe. My horse's ears pricked forward. His body tensed beneath me, electricity running through muscle and sinew. For a breath, we weren't separate; we were potential. No longer connected to the ground, but flying in formation with spiritual currents.

Haven's laugh broke through—pure, startled joy. I felt my own laugh rise, unbidden. A response to something larger than language. Larger than this moment.

The wild herd called to our ponies, "Where are you going?"

And ours responded with urgency, "Home! Will you run with us?"

"We will for a time."

And run they did. And I was there. Caught up in their motion. Forgetting for that little space that I was only a human and not some mystical being of horse and wind and wild song.

They did eventually peel away with soft nickers of goodbye. I craned my neck to watch them drop behind and consider us briefly before returning to their grazing.

And still, we fast-trotted, relentlessly churning through the kilometers. I was solidly back on earth, no longer distracted and soaring, but bouncing and trying not to. Holding on, while trying not to hold too tightly. Eyes straining for obstacles yards ahead because any closer, and I wouldn't have enough time to react.

When we did pause, I just looked wide-eyed at Carly, and she said one word breathlessly: "Grueling!"

Yes, grueling! Hadn't I fantasized about this? This wide-open land where you could go on and on and on and not stop? It was amazing. It was exhausting. The pause wasn't near long enough. Soon we were back at it.

My mind drifted in random directions. I remember thinking about something Julie had said. How when you come to a situation like this, where no one knows you, you can be whoever you want to be. Remake yourself. And I thought, *who has the energy for that? I am too exhausted to be anything else but me.* All pretenses dropped. For better or worse, my authentic self was making an appearance. I wondered if I would like her.

A snake slithered across my path, shocking me back to the present. A ginormous bird launched into the air, bigger than any bird I have ever even heard of outside of fantasy, and I decided it must have been the inspiration for a griffin (half-lion, half-eagle). A fox watched me from a distance, its keen eyes tracking, maybe hoping our thundering hooves would draw out a gopher meal for him.

I wanted to talk about these things at break but found that words were not coming easily. Instead, we all just collapsed in a puddle of shared exhaustion upon one blanket that Julie laid out for us—a "cuddle puddle," if you will. We fit everyone on it, lying this way and that. Close together and close to the ground, where we got a break from the relentless wind. There was something healing in physical touch, a source of warmth and an energy transfer, even when it is simply shoulders pressed against shoulders on a crowded blanket. In these moments, our individual exhaustion seemed to dissipate, shared and softened by our proximity. I listened to our collective breathing and sought peace. I wasn't going through this alone, and that brought deep comfort. I may have fallen asleep for a moment. I may have even snored.

One thing surprised me repeatedly. On each leg of the journey, I rode to the point that I simply could not imagine going another step. In the gym, we call this the *failure point.* When your muscles simply cannot lift the weight one more time. Like a car running out of gas. It was a hard stop.

Out in the desert, someone would call a break, and I would somehow dismount and stumble over to the blanket and collapse, convinced I would never get back up again. But after a few moments rest and some time with my team, I would take a deep breath and realize I probably could go a little farther. So, then, up I would get to do it all over again.

Sitting up, my hand found a small rock. I picked it up and held it. Just a little rock, but it felt grounding and significant. I decided to keep it, so I put it in the van.

At lunch, we had a longer break, and it was then, after refueling with sandwiches, that I found the energy to mention the snake.

"I saw one, too!" Carly said.

"What direction was it traveling?" asked Julie.

"I have no idea?" I said. "Which way is north?"

"No, I mean, was it heading left or right?"

I thought about it for a moment. "Left," I said, while Carly said "Right." "Why?" we both asked.

"If a creature passes you going left, it is a symbol that it is entering your deel, which is the only direction you can enter it from. This is a symbol of coming wealth. If it passes going right, it is leaving your deel, and that is a symbol of coming bad luck."

I was not sure a snake in my deel was good luck in any scenario, but I was willing to take whatever luck there was to be had. However, my good luck turned bad at the afternoon break, when Julie came to our group to translate for Bayaraa, the driver of the van.

"Whoever put the rock in the van, please remove it right away," she said sternly.

Turns out, picking rocks and sticks with the intention of keeping them as souvenirs is extremely bad luck. The earth is a body, and she doesn't like it when you take her parts.

The last stretch of the day was both the best and the worst. The end was in sight but still felt almost unattainable until we crested a small hill, and there in the distance, I saw the glorious orange-and-yellow domes of our tents. It had been a rough day. I was exhausted. I slid off my horse with only one thought: *That's Day Three, over and done. It will get easier from here.* I should have knocked on wood right then and there.

Instead, I trudged to the evening campfire and dropped contentedly onto the canvas chair that waited. Haven was already there. Soon Carly arrived, looking relieved. And, finally,

Brandon, with his medicine bag, which he proceeded to rummage through.

"That was rough," I said.

"Yeah," Carly agreed.

"Did you see those birds? What were they called?"

"I'm calling them 'griffins,'" Haven said confidently, and my heart swelled.

The evening settled on us like a sweet blanket. As had become our custom, Carly asked her thought-provoking question for the day.

"Do you fear failure?"

We all considered this.

"I guess I do," I said. "I'm a little afraid that I won't be able to finish this ride."

The others looked at me, and I shrugged. It was true. I was worried that my horse would trip and I would be crushed. And even if that didn't happen, I was worried that I wasn't tough enough. That one afternoon, I would just give it all up and demand they send me home in the van.

Carly clarified. "I mean, in life. Not just here."

And I reflected that my answer was the same. I was afraid that I wasn't tough enough for any of it. But as I sat there, surrounded by these people who were strangers just days ago, I realized that failure wasn't what truly terrified me. It was an entirely different fear that took root years ago, on an entirely different journey. A journey that started with a phone call to reserve a moving van.

Road Trip!

Bags packed? Check. Fuel in the tank? Check. Grandma strapped down? Mom tucked in her corner? Check and Check.

It was a sunny day in 2016, and two days before, I had called to reserve the moving truck. The lady taking my reservation asked, "What are you hauling?"

I wasn't prepared to answer that question. "Do I have to tell you?" I asked.

There was complete silence on the other end.

"That sounded pretty sketchy, huh?" I asked.

"Yes," the lady said.

So, I told her. "My sister and I are hauling my dead grandmother back to North Dakota for her funeral."

Silence again.

"That didn't help, did it?" I asked.

"Um, no," she said.

I could sense no laughter in this woman, but I hoped that at the end of the day, she went home and told her family all about it. "You'll never guess the conversation I had today," I imagined her saying.

I didn't mention that we were also hauling our mother's ashes.

The previous year, our mother had died of metastasized breast cancer. Last week, our grandmother died of old age. We were taking them both back to Stanley, North Dakota, to bury them side by side in the family plot.

A moving van wasn't our first choice for this endeavor. The train was considered, but new regulations insisted that we drive two hours to the nearest ticketed station. The same was true for an airplane. I could only imagine the stress of pulling into the departure lane at Seatac to unload my grandma in her cardboard travel coffin and deliver her to checked baggage. I'd probably have to rent one of those wheeled carts. In the end, it just made the most sense to rent a moving van.

The moving van lady may not have had laughter in her, but I had it in me in spades. Laughter, along with anger, peace, sorrow, and joy, all moved into my internal living room and made themselves comfortable. These competing emotions set aside their differences and had become fast friends. Sometimes, they all got to talking at once, creating a cacophony so loud that all I could do was sit and stare, usually out a window, sometimes with tears running down my face.

"You got the story?" my little sister asked.

"Check," I said, as I pulled up the audio book.

This road trip to North Dakota was the same annual 2,000-mile trip we took as kids, and we would sing "Over the river and through the woods, to Grandmother's house we go."

Grandma lived all but the last few years of her life in North Dakota, coming to Washington only when she could no longer care for herself. She was a prairie girl, used to the silence and wind. To sit with her was to sit in the eye of the storm: peaceful and calm.

My mother, a nurse, was the logical choice of Grandma's five children when Grandma needed full-time care. Mom spent her adult life riding an emotional roller coaster. To sit with her was to be tossed by the storm: restless and sometimes volatile.

I looked at my sister. She was beautiful, but she didn't know it. She was tough as nails, but so tender that I was scared of hurting her. She was the warrior you'd want at your side.

Grandma was peace, Mom was adventure, my sister was courage, and I—I was afraid of being left alone.

My mother was afraid of a lot of things, but she was not afraid of death. Her favorite thing to say was, "I'm in a win-win situation! If I live, I get to stay with you guys—win! If I die, I get to go home to Jesus—win!"

That was fine for her. But where was my win? When she passed away, the only thing I got was a living room full of emotions and more responsibility.

My first decision as the newly appointed most highly functioning matriarch was to move Grandma into memory care. On moving day, she was in fine form, my little cutie in her big sunglasses and pink pantsuit, ready for an outing. She didn't really understand what was going on, just that it was all about her. We got her settled, and then it was time to leave her there. It was a cozy room. The place smelled nice. But she looked so small. She must have sensed my unease, because she smiled at me and thanked me for the visit. Then she said she thought she might nap.

And here, a year later, she was strapped down in the back of a moving van. These were my thoughts as we pulled out into traffic.

My sister and I, the two living members of this adventure party, listened to our story, a murder mystery, and whenever we stopped, we talked about what we thought might happen next. And as soon as we finished our food, gas fill-up, or picture-taking, we raced back to the truck to hear the next chapter.

We watched the most amazing thunder and lightning storm move across the prairie.

We took pictures of fence lines, oil wells, buffalo, and old barns. We drove through the Badlands, which, while beautiful, would never be as beautiful as my mother's description of them.

When the road was bumpy, I worried that our passengers were getting jostled, which was ridiculous, I knew this. What did they care? But still...

We stopped late in a hotel whose hot tub had closed for the night. My sister insisted we go anyway and hopped over the fence. She slid into the steaming water and looked back at me. "What is taking you so long?" she asked.

I considered my little sister. We were so much alike: both messed up and both sort of badass. And I thought, *I'm hauling two dead bodies in the back of a moving van. What's a little trespassing?* Responsibility scooted over to give recklessness room on the couch.

An idea had been creeping up on me all day, and when I joined my sister, it peeked out at me. The idea had to do with my "win." It had to do with being so incredibly thankful for this moment and for my sister, and for my mother and my grandmother. It had to do with the circle of life. And...

And then the idea slipped back into the shadows. It wasn't ready for the light, but it left behind contentment, who smiled at the room and said, "All right, everyone, it's time to settle down. We have work to do."

Years later, sitting in a ger in Mongolia, surrounded by strangers who were becoming family, I understood that fear of failure wasn't what truly terrified me. It was the fear of being left behind. Alone. Losing Mom was hard. Losing Charlie was devastating. But somewhere between hauling my mother's ashes across North Dakota and riding across Mongolia's endless steppes, I learned something vital about survival: It's not about avoiding loss at all. It's simply a perspective shift.

We rode 70K on Day Three for a total of 186K, or 115 miles.

7
Day Four

False Hope

Date: September 14, 2022
Distance: 83K, or 52 miles

Day Four had started off so promising. I thought to myself, *The worst is behind me. It is only going to get better from here.* Then I started my morning routine: I got myself up and to the bathroom, but nothing came out. So, then I met Haven for Tai Chi.

Haven was an excellent and encouraging instructor. He demonstrated each motion, maneuvering so he was always in my line of sight. We completed our routine just as the others were emerging from their tents. My body felt better prepared to do this thing.

Then I went to the bathroom again. After the exercise, I was thinking things would move. Unfortunately, they didn't. I was starting to feel bloated.

Next up was packing my bags for the day. I tried to think of what all I needed, but it was a little difficult. So, I zipped the bag closed and hoped for the best.

I went to the bathroom again, and now I was feeling frustrated. I trudged back to the tent for breakfast. On the way, Bayaraa looked at me with concern in his eyes.

Breakfast happened and I ate as much as I could.

Bayaraa came into the breakfast tent and talked to Julie. Julie turned to me. "He wants to make sure I know you might not be feeling great."

"He's right," I said.

And now everyone was paying attention. I told them I hadn't been able to poop, and I felt like I had to pee all the time, but nothing was coming out. I said these exact words. To my entire team. And I was laughing a little because it seemed a little surreal to be talking about these very personal things with people I just met four days ago. But there it was.

"I have something for that!" Brandon proclaimed, and he ran to grab his medical bag. Haven raised an eyebrow and quietly went to his tent. They both returned with treatments. I worried that Brandon's approach might be too effective. I opted for Haven's silver-colored pill, even though it looked strange to me. Haven promised it would help my system "gently" regulate. Tom encouraged me to make sure I was drinking water. Everyone wanted me to eat more. Altitude sickness, heat sickness, and bladder infection were all on the table.

Lhaagva approached and told me through Julie that he wanted to try a Mongolian treatment. "When your belly is hurting, keep it warm." And he took the long, silk belt from my deel and wrapped me up tightly. I pulled my fleece coat over the top and felt pretty snug.

Julie brought me a hat to protect my head from the sun and heat. It was a ridiculous hat, floppy and old lady style. Made so that you could roll it up and throw it in your luggage. I considered it with trepidation and then looked at Haven with a question in my eyes.

"You should wear it," he said. "It will protect you from the sun, which could be part of why you aren't feeling good. You are at a significant altitude change from home. That combined with nearly constant sun exposure could be causing quicker dehydration, heat exhaustion, headaches from squinting, and, um, everything else."

Just a couple days ago, I was riding with my hair flying in the wind and a sports bra. Now I was bundled up like an old lady. Sigh. I put the hat on. And then I had to tie it down so it wouldn't blow away. So now I had a bonnet. I looked at Haven again.

"You look great!" he said, getting to the heart of my concern. Vanity—it was a real thing. I decided to pretend he was telling the truth.

And then we were mounting for our first 20K of the day. That's how they attempted to break it down for us: 20K, then a break, 20K, then lunch, 15K, another break, and then after 15K, stop for the night. Of course, this was only the goal—all of the days were adjusted according to the needs of that day. Still, four segments with breaks between were like bite-sized pieces of an enormous task. Twenty kilometers to the first break felt doable. Thinking about the full 70 that lay ahead was overwhelming, so I focused on just this first stretch as we headed out.

The morning air felt different—the relentless wind had finally taken a breath, giving us a rare moment of calm. The field before us was of lumpy grass, its green a stark contrast to the golden-brown steppes we'd been crossing for days. My horse's hooves made soft thuds against the springy earth, so different from the hard-packed ground we'd grown used to.

Carly rode beside me, close enough that we could actually talk without shouting, for once. We exchanged quips about ridiculous hats, our laughter carrying easily in the still air. The sun felt gentle on my face, more like a friend than the harsh taskmaster it had been (maybe this damn hat was a good idea, after all), and I dared to hope that today might be better than yesterday.

That's when the screaming started.

Actually, *screaming* wasn't the right word for what was happening. Julie Veloo was too tough a person to just "scream." She released a torrent of cuss words in an explosive expulsion of air that started with surprise and ended in pure anger. I turned around when it first started and watched as Julie's horse stumbled to the ground, attempted to lurch up, but going down again, this time rolling with Julie somewhere in the midst of the chaos, yelling her head off. Baagii, who had been in front of us, raced past us to reach her in moments. Carly and I scanned the horizon for the medical van. For once, it wasn't anywhere near us. This ground was not passable by vehicle, and they were instead taking the long way around. Apparently, that also meant they weren't looking our way. Carly and I began to race toward it, waving our arms and shouting until the headlights flashed, letting us know they'd spotted us, and the van turned off the road to meet us by Julie.

Tom jumped out of the van and raced to her side. The cussing had stopped by this point, and dammit if she wasn't laughing. And Baagii was yelling at her. Julie must have seen my face, because she explained that this was how she knew Baagii loved her. He was mad that she wasn't paying attention. He was telling her that this was her fault.

I guess I can relate to that kind of love. When a child is lost, and you are scared to death, and then when you find them, your first response is extreme relief, but your second response is anger: "What were you thinking! You need to stay where I can see you!"

I felt a little like Baagii, except that I wasn't convinced she was OK yet. She didn't look OK to me. Tom examined her and then helped her to her feet. They decided nothing was broken, and Julie got back on her horse.

Soon, Baagii was laughing, too, and teasing her, and we were on our way again.

I was shook, though, and I rode in silence, worried about this. If Julie, with all her experience, had been thrown, it was only a matter of time until I would be. Mounting and dismounting were already painful when the horse was standing still, each movement sending sharp protests through my joints. How much worse would it be to fly off, uncontrolled and unexpectedly?

After about an hour, we were riding along a dirt road when we spotted two gers, the traditional round dwellings of Mongolia's nomads, sitting on the side of the road. Their white canvas walls stretched taut over a lattice of curved wooden poles, the whole structure cinched at the waist by a band of rope and crowned with a wooden wheel open to the sky. Smoke drifted from the central hole in their steeply pitched roofs, promising warmth within.

A woman outside spotted us. She shouted something and dashed into one of the gers. Moments later, she emerged with a man carrying a plate of food. He signaled for us to stop, his weathered face breaking into a welcoming smile. They offered us hard cheese and plain yogurt for dipping, approaching each rider carefully, mindful of our horses. Our guides exchanged soft words with them while we fumbled shy thank-yous. When they reached me, the man insisted I take several pieces, his earnest generosity making refusal impossible. I tucked them into my sleeve for later, touched by this moment of connection in the vast emptiness.

The moment felt profound. Like we were actors in a scene that had played out for centuries—the famed Mongolian hospitality. I thought I understood it. I could imagine that when you spend your life surrounded by this endless land, the isolation of it, the loneliness of it, creates a craving for human interaction. Travelers were not just tolerated; they were welcomed with openness and let go with reluctance. "Please stay awhile. Tell us what you know, where you have been, where you are going." Their eagerness reflected an ancient yearning: "Help us to see what is in the world beyond this."

I had traveled halfway around the world seeking adventure in their everyday life. To them, *this* was normal. This was routine. This was their world, day in and day out. We were the adventure, visitors to be stared at and wondered over.

In spite of Julie's accident, the morning took a hopeful turn. At our first break, I actually felt hungry, which was a welcome change. The peanuts looked innocent enough, their sweet coating glistening. I should have known better, should have checked what that coating was, but I grabbed handful after handful, caught up in the simple pleasure of appetite.

The sickness hit just as the break ended. Brandon caught my expression before I even realized my face had changed. "I have something for that," he offered, already reaching for his medical kit. I waved him off—this nausea was an old friend, a souvenir from that stomach surgery years ago. Eating too quickly, especially anything sweet, was a combination my modified digestive system rejected with predictable vengeance. Usually thirty minutes of misery, then it'd be done. I could handle that.

I mounted up, clinging to the certainty that I'd feel better by lunch. But the next 20K had other plans. The muscle pain I'd hoped would ease after day three returned with reinforcements. Each transition from trot to canter drew a muttered "Shit, here we go again" through gritted teeth. My right leg, once reliable, began to betray me. The steady rhythm needed to move as one with the horse slipped away, replaced by jerky compensation and growing dread.

In that moment of weakness, my personal monsters made their first appearance.

Monsters

"You don't matter."

"You don't matter."

"No one likes you."

"You are a fake."

"You are weak."

"You suck."

"Sucks."

"Sucks."

The words hammered at me in four-count rhythm, as steady and merciless as my horse's hooves against the earth, each impact jarring both body and mind. My monsters whispered, sang, and shouted, an endless chorus of doubt wrapped in nonstop, creative cruelty. They spoke things I knew were not true, yet some part of me believed them with absolute certainty.

I tried to fight back with self talk.

"You're OK."

"You got this."

But my voice came out weak, beaten down by exhaustion and pain. I was weak.

"You are weak."

"You are weak."

Through the fog of doubt and endless wind, I remembered Chance, my trainer at the gym, standing over me at the rowing machine. "Harder! Faster!" I felt like I was giving everything I had, and it wasn't enough.

"I'm just a wimp," I'd said.

Chance had looked me straight in the eye. "You. Are. No. Wimp."

"I am strong!" I shouted back to the monsters, my hands tightening on the reins until my knuckles whitened.

"Lies!" the monsters hissed.

"Ya Ho Va Way," I whispered, the ancient syllables carrying more strength than my words.

"That's not even a word," they mocked.

"Ya Ho Va Way," I said again, remembering how breath itself can be prayer. Each inhale a reminder that I was held, each exhale a surrender.

"God can't help you," they sneered.

"Ya Ho Va Way." I called to the same God who had walked with me through grief and who was here on the steppe, present in every breath.

"What in the world do you expect God to do right now? Foolish naïve child! You put yourself in this situation."

"You asked for this."

"You deserve this."

"YA HO VA WAY!!!"

Teeth-Gritted Endurance

When we stopped for lunch, I slid painfully off my horse. The urgent bathroom trek yielded nothing, so I stumbled back to our community blanket and collapsed.

Visitors came, their voices a distant murmur I could not focus on. I lay in silent misery with Carly, Brandon, and Haven. When lunch appeared, I couldn't force it past my throat. Small pieces of granola were all I could manage. Then, before we were ready, it was time to mount up.

That's when we heard the cursing. Julie's voice, sharp with pain.

We gathered around her. "What's wrong?"

"I don't know!" she gasped, bent over.

But I thought I knew. Back spasms, the body's cruel response to trauma—like, say, being thrown from a horse. If you've never experienced one, count yourself lucky. The pain shoots through you like lightning, leaving you breathless and shaken. Julie had simply tried to stand up from sitting on the ground, and her back had betrayed her.

Tom's inspection led to the inevitable: She needed to take a break from riding. Julie bristled at the suggestion but didn't argue. The logistics shuffle: Tom had to take a horse so Julie could ride in the van. Once again, Carly volunteered to take Julie's Mongolian saddle, letting Tom use her English-Western cross.

We headed out for our first 15K of the afternoon. My monster battle paused, replaced by worry for Julie. What if she's done serious damage? What if she is too tough to admit how bad it is? I looked ahead at Baagii, riding relentlessly forward. He never looked back, and I was pretty sure he didn't care whether we followed. What if we were left with only Baagii to watch out for us?

At the afternoon break, we were told that Julie had relented and they were taking her to the hospital. And, therefore, our route had been modified to follow her there. In fact, we would meet a driver at one end of town who would take us to a store. A store! Where we could buy anything we might need.

What did I need? What would help? I tried to put my counting mind to work on that.

Everyone was in good spirits at the thought of the store, but I was still feeling pretty awful, and my mind was sluggish. More toilet paper, I decided. And what else? Oh, a proper hat! My own brush! And then, finally, I thought, *I bet they have a bathroom here.* And when I voiced that thought, Carly perked right up. We were told it was on the second floor.

A real bathroom felt like an impossible luxury, even if my body still refused to cooperate. I caught my reflection at the sink and froze.

The woman in the mirror was a different color than I'd ever seen before—deeply tanned and layered in dust, and somehow more red. Her lips were chapped and swollen. She was a woman who had been through some stuff. I stared hard and then gave her a tentative smile.

I was taken aback. *Oh, there you are!* I thought. As if I had lost myself somewhere on the trail.

I remembered Carly saying, "I only have the clothes I have." And I thought now, *I only have the face I have.* And whatever my opinion of it, this is the face of a woman who decided to go to Mongolia and ride 700K in 10 days. I kinda liked her.

The stairs on our way out proved treacherous on our exhausted legs. When Carly slipped and fell several feet, I froze in panic—until she burst out laughing.

"I come all the way to Mongolia," she gasped between fits of giggles, "ride in the longest annual charity ride, and get hurt falling down the stairs on my way back *from the bathroom!*"

Soon we were both doubled over, the absurdity of it all breaking through our exhaustion.

More Questions

That evening, tired but somehow lighter, we gathered for our nightly ritual of conversation. We listened to Julie recount her hospital visit. They had given her some pain medicine and sent her on her way. I was so thankful she would be riding with us again.

Brandon posed the evening question: what did our names mean? We had a rare evening of cell service and we used that precious signal to google and find out.

Carly's name meant free woman, independent-minded, friendly, and compassionate.

Julie's was youthful or vivacious.

Rachael's was ewe, little lamb.

Brandon's was prince or king.

Haven's was safe and comfortable. But Haven is his middle name so we asked him what his first name, "Kenneth," meant, and he said with a shrug, "I don't know. Big nose or something like that." I googled it. Kenneth meant "handsome." I teased him about it, but he was clearly uncomfortable. I dropped it.

Tuya was delivering our food and we asked her, "What does your name mean?" And she responded "Ray of sun," which described her perfectly.

I was astounded by how appropriately each of us had been named.

And then we talked about our travels. We had all been places. What was the one thing we tried to buy wherever we go?

Haven said he tries to find a cultural mask. He had a display at home of them all. He was fascinated by the similarity—each one was a mask—and by their diversity—each mask was distinct.

I looked for mugs. I like to drink my morning coffee and revisit places I've been.

Carly picked up Christmas ornaments. They were small and portable. And every year, as she placed them on her tree, she got to relive the memories.

And then we went deep: "What is your biggest fear?" This

question struck differently than the one the other night about fearing failure.

I am afraid that my monsters might be right, I thought, but I didn't share that out loud. I had thought being left alone was what scared me most, but now, riding through Mongolia's endlessness with these incredible people, I realized something worse: the possibility that I might deserve to be alone. That my monsters spoke the truth when they said I didn't matter.

I Can't Do This

That fear wasn't born in Mongolia. It had taken root in the aftermath of Charlie's death, when even the simplest tasks became monuments to loss. One afternoon, while cleaning the stables, I found myself drowning in the endless list of things I now faced alone: mow the lawn, fix the door handle (first figure out how), remember to feed the dog, vacuum, wash dishes, actually ride my horse. Each task carried Charlie's ghost—his laugh, his way of doing things, the space where he should have been.

Spring came, and I started having trouble with Roan, my beautiful quarter horse. He was my first horse that I could call mine since Breezy. He came into my life the summer of 2020 in a sort of roundabout way. I liked to say I inherited him, but the more accurate story was that my sister inherited him, and she gifted him to me. He had been our stepdad, Bud's, last horse. When Bud passed away in his eighties, Becky became Roan's full owner, but she was not in a position to have a horse. I looked at Charlie, and he said, "Let's make it work!"

Now, this beautiful horse was another source of pain, reminding me how much I had lost. If you know anything about horses, then you will not be surprised I started having behavior issues with him.

The first time it happened, I'd ridden him a little way off the stable grounds. He started fine, but his anxiety steadily climbed until it felt like he was going to bolt on me. I was doing everything I knew to do to calm him, but I was also getting angry, and soon I knew we both needed a break. I thought I should get off and just lead him around, which I did, but he still was being ridiculous. So, I thought I'd just tie him up for a moment and get some space. He jerked his head back and broke the rein and ran back to the barn without me.

I did the Cowgirl Walk of Shame back to the barn and arrived just as they were sending out a car to look for me.

This behavior continued. I asked his vet to come and look him over. Maybe he was in pain. The vet said he was in excellent shape, that this wasn't a physical problem. He suggested a horse trainer.

I met with a horse trainer who had worked with Roan in his youth. She spent an hour with him. She said, "He seems OK. This might be a rider problem."

She recommended a person who trains people.

I called that person up. She was too busy to take me on, but we talked. And something she said gave me a clue.

They say that horses are in tune with your emotions. I always believed that, but I didn't really understand what that meant. What it seemed to mean in our case was that Roan was feeling all the things I was feeling, but for him, he didn't have a source for these emotions. I was bringing him a storm cloud of fear, feelings of being overwhelmed, and anxiety. He felt he was going to be attacked at any moment.

Once I realized what I was doing, I stopped. Instead, I focused on staying in the moment. The comforting smell of my horse. The creak of the saddle. I said out loud, "You don't have to worry about a thing, Roan. I've got you. I'm going to keep you safe." I said it with my words, and I said it with my body language, even when I didn't believe it myself.

And sometimes, in the quiet moments between my reassurances to Roan, I sensed God doing the same for me, speaking peace into my storm even when I wasn't ready to hear it. Like a parent soothing a frightened child, presence was enough.

And it was like night and day with Roan's behavior. When he started acting up again, I learned to do a self-scan. What was I feeling? Every single time, I was having my own emotional storm. If I could, I would dial it back. If I couldn't, then I would be done riding for the day.

Slowly, over time, things got easier. Going on without Charlie wasn't my choice, and it wasn't fun, but it was possible. Slowly, dreams I had set aside began to make noise again. Dreams like riding in the longest annual charity ride on the planet.

But now I was here, muscles aching, spirit wavering, and I wondered if it had been a mistake to come—if I had finally found the limit of what I could endure.

We covered 83K on Day Four, for a total of 269K, or 167 miles.

8

Day Five

The Fall

Date: September 15, 2022
Distance: 67K, or 42 miles

> "You wake up every morning to fight the same demons that
> left you so tired the night before, and that, my love, is bravery."
>
> —Author unknown

Day Five crept in like an unwelcome guest. My body, now operating on this new schedule, yanked me awake at 5:30 a.m. with the familiar urgent need for the bathroom. This time, finally: blessed relief. I emptied out and the bloating decreased, though now I was worried about the opposite of constipation.

Dawn painted the steppe in watercolors—pale pinks bleeding into soft blues—as I met Haven for our morning Tai Chi. The air still carried the night's chill, our breath visible in small clouds. I assumed my now-familiar starting pose when we were interrupted by Tom, who had jogged over to join us.

I wondered if he was going to. The night before, sitting in our evening circle, Brandon had said to Tom, "I will pay you $100 to do Tai Chi in the morning!"

I wasn't sure what inspired Brandon to do this. I hadn't been paying close attention to the bonding between Tom and Brandon. I was always the first to retreat to my tent each night. The days were brutal enough without adding exhaustion from late-night socializing. If I tried to do them without sleep, I would break. I was pretty close to breaking already. So, as much as I wanted to hang out with the "cool kids," I was usually the first to leave.

Haven and Carly reassured me I wasn't missing anything. In fact, Haven said, "I'm just waiting for you to go to bed so that I can excuse myself as well."

But Brandon and Tom hadn't done this. They frequently stayed up late into the night, drinking and talking. They made an odd pair: Tom, with his rough language and baseline dislike of humanity as a whole; and Brandon, with his Ivy League education, CEO status, and a job that required him to be liked by everyone he met. Relationships were Brandon's bread and butter. Tom, on the other hand, cared about only a few select individuals who had earned his respect. Everyone else could "go to hell."

I thought Brandon was intrigued by Tom's approach to life. It might have seemed like freedom in some ways.

Whatever was happening there, they were becoming fast friends. And, somehow, their conversations had led Brandon to throw down the gauntlet of "I will pay you $100 to do Tai Chi in the morning!" And so Tom did.

Haven's face tightened when Tom approached. Haven was a teacher and believer of Tai Chi. He didn't want to be a part of some drunken game. He didn't want his practice cheapened.

But Tom was respectful. He said in his rough way that he respected Tai Chi for its history. He had always been curious about it. And then asked to join in. Partway through, Haven took off his shirt. This was pretty routine for him because he ran hot. Tom looked at me and smiled encouragingly, and I laughed.

"This is not topless Tai Chi, sorry," I told him.

Tom grinned, shrugged in an "it was worth a shot" kind of motion, and we continued through the movements.

Brandon bore witness and, at the end, handed Tom $100. Tom then turned to Haven with the $100. Haven said, "Donate it to the foundation." And that was how Haven continued to fundraise even after the ride had started.

We mounted up, and I found myself on Kevin Smith, Haven's Goth horse. I was excited! "Good morning, handsome!" I said to him, but he was indifferent. "Whatever," he said back to me. I was not offended.

We headed out on our first 20K (that's about 12.5 miles), and we were maybe 2K into it when Kevin Smith's front legs buckled. He went down on both front knees, and the ground rushed up at an impossible angle. Time stretched like taffy—slow enough to see the dirt coming at my face, fast enough that there was no time to be afraid. My body moved on pure instinct, hands snapping tight on the reins, legs braced forward in my stirrups. Lhaagva's alarmed cry cut through the morning air.

I somehow kept my seat, and when I was upright again, we made eye contact, and he gave me an approving nod and a smile. I had pulled a groin muscle. And now trotting was torture, but I felt a glow from Lhaagva's approval. Plus, I didn't get rolled. Soon the pulled muscle relaxed and I was back in stride.

I was a little in awe, actually. The thing I feared had happened. It happened so fast. And now it was over.

Maybe it is going to be OK?

Mongolia!

It was like riding through painting after painting. Epic landscapes with horses: my favorite kind of painting! And I was in it. That little dot right there? That's me!

It was like time travel. Genghis Khan in Baagii form leading us. And we were the horde, following our leader, trying to be fierce.

It was like being inside a legend—not just reading about great adventures, but living one, complete with aching muscles and the constant taste of dust.

Carly had ear buds in, and when she saw me looking, she self-consciously explained, "I'm listening to an audio book about Genghis Khan. There is something really amazing about listening to this story in the actual setting that it took place!"

And I was a little jealous of her. What a terrific idea to quiet those internal thoughts of doubt.

Brandon was singing, his own ear buds on a playlist. This, too, seemed like a terrific idea. Haven also sang quietly. But my favorite was when Lhaagva broke into song. A Mongolian song—and did you know that in Mongolia, there are more songs about horses than there are about love? His tenor voice swept me up, carrying centuries of history across the steppe.

And then Kevin Smith went down again. Same sequence: buckled knees, lurching ground, automatic reaction, another groin pull, another approving nod from Lhaagva. But this time, the fear lingered after I was upright.

I asked Lhaagva if Kevin Smith was OK. I said the words in English, but I gestured to my horse and tried to express my concern in his direction. Lhaagva rode around me and then nodded, indicating that Kevin Smith was fine. I wanted to believe him, but Kevin Smith went down two more times before break. Each time, my confidence took the same hit as my body.

By now, my hands were shaking on the reins, my muscles tense with anticipation of the next fall. When I told Julie, "My horse is tripping a lot! Can you get them to look him over?" I was trying to not sound as desperate as I felt.

Baagii's verdict didn't help: Kevin Smith was just bored. He wasn't paying attention. I needed to have a firmer hand with him.

Watching Baagii dismiss my concerns pissed me off, but I wasn't voicing my concerns correctly, which had always been my problem. He thought I was just asking whether Kevin Smith was OK. Which Baagii answered: Yes, he is. But what I was really saying was, I didn't want to be on a horse that I couldn't trust. Charlie would have understood this. He would have known what I meant. But he wasn't here and I only had myself.

OK, I thought, but exhaustion had hollowed out any resolve I might have had. *After lunch, I'll be firmer, whatever that means.* The constant vigilance was wearing me down faster than the physical pain. My leg pains from the first days hadn't let up. The dam had broken and things were coming out of me fast. I could hardly get any food down, and now I had a torn groin muscle. Each fall chipped away at what little strength I had left.

I lay down on the group blanket and fell asleep. After a bit, I got up to find a place to go to the bathroom, and Haven said, "Look at you all walking around and stuff." I smiled gratefully at him. I was not alone. He was also too tired and sore to move unless absolutely needed.

Brandon was standing to the side of the blanket, and he had his hand down his pants, rubbing vigorously. He was so blatant about it that I just watched, confused about what I was seeing. He saw me and just said, "Chafing." And that's when I noticed the ointment in his other hand. Ah, OK.

Julie leaned against the truck. Her face looked ashen, and I knew she was in pain. We all were. But Julie's pain was scarier to me. I didn't have faith that she would stop unless she was dead. I thought maybe she just needed permission to take a break. I made a statement, "You know, we will be OK if you decide to ride in the truck."

This was a lie. We would *not* be OK if she decided to ride in the truck. She was our advocate out there. The one keeping track of the miles. The one insisting we slow the pace at least once in a while. I didn't trust Baagii. He was cold and indifferent. If we were left with only him, I thought I could be run into the ground and left for dead.

But I was thinking she might be trying to be "tough" for us.

She said, "Will you be offended if I say 'Fuck off'?"

I actually was offended, and it surprised me. But Julie had no idea what my statement cost me. She had no idea that the idea of her not riding with us filled me with panic, and it was only because my concern for her outweighed my concern for myself that I even suggested it.

But I also recognized that she wasn't just telling me to fuck off. She was telling the pain and her own weakness to fuck off. She wouldn't go down that easily.

I turned away and let her fight her own battle. My own monsters needed attending.

In the 15K after lunch, Kevin Smith went down three more times. I found myself sitting in an awkward hunched-over position, trying to protect everything that hurt: my body, my pride, my dwindling confidence. Each step became a silent prayer that we'd stay upright.

Julie rode up beside me and said, "Would you look at that horse's mane?" She was indicating a horse that was running free and had decided to run with us for a bit. Where had it even come from? I looked up and saw we were again surrounded by free-range horses. They ran beside us, some with heads high, others with heads stretched forward. They moved smoothly, like a school of fish moves, as one. Beneath their horsehair coats, their muscles rippled, and their hooves hit the ground in rhythmic waves. These horses and our horses flowed over the land, and I was swept away. This was magic! And I was missing it.

Now I tried to focus on the horse that Julie indicated.

She continued, "There are so many colors! I didn't even know that many colors existed, let alone in a horse's mane."

And I was in awe of her.

Julie got on a horse for the first time when she was fifty years old. And now her life was riding horses. She had already put 5,000K on horseback that year alone. She was riding the toughest ride I'd ever been on, and she was doing it with pulled back muscles, laughing and taking pictures the whole time.

When she rode away from me, I stole some of her grit. *I will get through this,* I thought.

•   •   •

Just after break, Kevin Smith went down again. He came up, and I was in tears. I looked at Carly and said, "This is getting old!" And she said, "Ask for a different horse."

Of course! I could just ask for a different horse. The solution was so obvious, yet it hadn't even occurred to me. I had been enduring, pushing through, making do, my default response to everything since losing Charlie. But Carly's five words cut through all that. I found Julie and told her, straight out: "I need a different horse. I have pulled my groin muscle and I can't take this anymore."

So, she rode up and stopped Baagii. We all dismounted, and they took my saddle off Kevin Smith. But then they put Haven's saddle on him, and they gave me Haven's horse. I didn't want Haven to get hurt, either!

But Baagii said Kevin Smith would do better with a man riding him. I didn't know what that meant, and I was not reassured.

About 10K later, Haven went down. Kevin Smith landed on both front knees and then clambered back up. I was behind him when it happened, close enough to see it in horrifying detail. The impact rippled through Haven's body like a shock wave, starting at his hips where they met the saddle, rolling up through his spine in a perfect S-curve, and snapping out through his shoulders. It was like watching a snake move in slow motion, each vertebra following the one before in an impossible dance of survival. His body found angles I didn't know were possible, yet somehow he stayed centered, never losing his seat.

He looked at me grimly and said he was OK, but I wasn't sure I believed him. The image of that fluid, serpentine movement stayed with me, a master class in staying mounted when everything goes wrong.

More Than Just Sitting

After watching Haven's masterful recovery on Kevin Smith, you might be wondering, *How hard can riding really be? The horse is doing all the work, right? All you're doing is sitting.*

You wouldn't be the first to wonder this. In fact, I had a friend ask me this before I left. It was a legit question. I want to try to give you an idea.

I think riding a horse is the closest thing we have in the real world to riding dragons. Horses are incredible animals, with opinions on how they want to spend their time, and it isn't necessarily with you. Like dragons, they could be magnificent partners or dangerous adversaries. The difference comes down to how well you could dance together.

Like any partnership, it requires good communication, and communication with a horse is part physical and part emotional.

Physical communication is the whole body. You are signaling your requests by your posture, your legs, your hands, your arms, your feet, and even the direction you are pointing your head. All of your body has to be sending the same message all the time. Like when Kevin Smith stumbled, my hands had to tighten on the reins while my legs braced forward, all in perfect coordination. One wrong move and I'd have been eating dirt instead of earning Lhaagva's approving nod.

This requires being fully present *all the time*. If you want to get better at "staying in the moment," go horseback riding. There's no zoning out when you're scanning for gopher holes while managing a bored horse who'd rather be anywhere else.

Also, a rider is not just sitting. They are in tune with the horse's movement. Constant small muscle adjustments allow the rider to match the movement of their horse. I saw this in Haven every day, the way he seemed to float in that Mongolian saddle, moving as one with his mount. Watching a good rider on their horse is like watching two dancers. It is beautiful. Everything is in sync, graceful, and they appear to be moving as one. Even when a horse makes an unexpected move, such as a stumble, a buck, or a spook, a good rider who is paying attention is not fazed. It is just part of the dance. That's what I witnessed in Haven's impossible recovery—that fluid, serpentine movement that turned potential disaster into a masterclass in horsemanship.

And all this requires incredible muscle tone, flexibility, and balance. Think cross sport, plus ballet, plus Tai Chi. No wonder my morning Tai Chi sessions with Haven felt like essential preparation rather than just exercise.

Now, add the emotional elements. They say a horse is very aware of your emotions. I never really believed that until I rode Roan while grieving the loss of my Charlie. Every time I mounted up, Roan absorbed my storm of feelings—the overwhelming sadness, the anxiety about facing life alone, the moments of panic that would hit without warning. But, unlike me, Roan had no context for these emotions. He just knew something was terribly wrong, and it made him spooky and unpredictable. He'd start fine, but his anxiety would build until it felt like he was going to bolt. My grief was literally frightening my horse.

That's when I learned what people meant about horses being emotional mirrors. If I wanted to keep riding, I had to learn to compartmentalize, to acknowledge my feelings while projecting calm confidence for Roan's sake. "You don't have to worry about a thing," I'd tell him. "I've got you. I'm going to keep you safe." I had to say it with my words and show it with my body language, even when I didn't believe it myself.

A rider has to be aware of their emotional presence and in control. That's why so many cowboys and cowgirls are described as stoic. If you want someone who can appear calm when the shit is hitting the fan, then you want a horseback rider. It's not that we don't feel the fear or doubt; we just learn to package it away where our horses can't sense it.

So, when I say that riding horses requires your whole you, I mean your *whole you*: physical, mental, and emotional.

And riding an endurance ride requires all this, all day long, even when you are past exhausted. And then it means getting up the next day and doing it again. And then getting up the next day and doing it again. And continuing that for eleven days.

Each time Kevin Smith went down, it wasn't just testing my physical ability to stay mounted; it was draining my mental stamina and challenging my emotional control. Every stumble required me to overcome the fear of the last one, to project confidence I didn't feel, and to keep my body loose when everything in me wanted to tense up. And I still had days of riding ahead of me.

If I was going to finish this ride, it was going to take everything I had. And right now, after nine falls with Kevin Smith, I wasn't sure how much I had left.

Wait, Is Kevin Smith OK?

I didn't like riding a horse that tripped repeatedly, let alone one that went down on his front knees so often. Not only was it terrifying for me, but I couldn't imagine it was doing the horse any favors, either. Every time Kevin Smith stumbled, my stomach lurched with a mix of fear for myself and worry for him. His dark mane would sweep forward as his head dropped, the rhythm of his gait faltering without warning. Back home, a horse showing any sign of lameness would be pulled from riding immediately, probably seen by a vet, and definitely given time to rest. But here I was, watching Haven mount up on this horse after my turn with him, knowing he would likely go down again.

The worry gnawed at me. I was not a vet, nor did I have experience with endurance horses and what to look for if there was a problem. I looked at his feet, and they were well cared for, his hooves solid and shaped for the rocky terrain we traversed. So, I was out of ideas. What I did know was this:

First, Baagii had more experience with endurance horses than anyone I'd ever met. While I didn't trust Baagii to take care of me or make sure I made it out safely, I did trust him to know his horses.

He learned his trade from generations before him passing down their knowledge. You could see it in how his eyes constantly scanned the herd, noting each horse's movement, the way they carried themselves, how they interacted with others. When choosing horses for the ride, he told us, "While we are feeding and caring for our horses, we like to let them go on ordinary trips, which allows us to get to know each horse's behavior. For example, some horses look strong and active, but they are not. They are not ready for long-distance travel. We have to get to know each horse and its capabilities."

This wasn't just talk. I had seen proof. On Day One, we brought a beautiful tall, black horse that looked perfect for endurance riding—glossy coat catching the sun, muscles rippling with each step. But after just that first half-day, Baagii pulled him from the rotation. To my untrained eye, the horse still looked strong and healthy, but Baagii had seen something in his movement, some subtle sign that told him this horse wasn't ready for the demands ahead.

Second, Baagii matched horses to riders with careful consideration. I watched him study how each of us sat in the saddle, how we handled the reins, the way we moved with or against the horse's rhythm. "We mostly focus on choosing the right horse for riders," Baagii told us. "Horses' behaviors are so different. Some are speedy while some are gentle, and so we have to choose the right horse for each rider." When he said Kevin Smith was bored and got sleepy with a light rider, but did better with a man riding, he was speaking from deep observation and understanding.

Third, I watched how Baagii cared for the horses. He checked over them each evening, his weathered hands running down their legs, feeling for heat or swelling. Their legs were wrapped when needed, the white bandages stark against dark fur in the fading light. They were given vitamins and electrolytes, the ritual as natural as breathing for the crew. On rest day, every single horse got a thorough inspection, their eyes, ears, hooves, and joints all examined with quiet efficiency.

Fourth, and perhaps most important to understand, these

horses were not like the pampered horses I knew back home. They spent most of their time running free on the steppe, part of a herd that had to survive wolves and harsh weather. Where my trail horse Roan lived with regular meals and shelter, these horses lived by their wits and toughness. I'd seen it in how they moved across their native landscape, sure-footed in terrain that would terrify a domestic horse, strong enough to carry us through wind and weather that would keep most horses in their stables.

Just because they did things differently here didn't mean they did them wrong. In Mongolia, horses were both sacred and practical, revered in song and story, but expected to work. They were partners rather than pets, their strength respected rather than coddled. Still, Kevin Smith's stumbling was concerning. So I did my own research. The next time I had a signal, I googled, "Why is my horse tripping?" and one of the top answers was, "Your horse may stumble or trip if your horse is disinterested in his work," confirming what Baagii had said from the start.

Finally, I felt reassured. Kevin Smith, with his dark-gray coat and that long, black mane that covered his eyes like an equine emo kid, was indeed Goth down to his core—too bored and disaffected to even pick up his feet properly unless properly motivated. The explanation fit perfectly with everything I'd observed about his personality, from his indifferent ear flicks to his general air of "whatever" that somehow came through even when he was carrying us across the steppe.

Food

On the evening of Day Five, Zulaa came to the shelter they had put up so that we could have a break from the wind. His face held the same excited energy he'd shown when hauling our deels on the first day. He made an announcement with a dramatic flourish:

"Tonight, we have something very special for you. The chef has made you a special treat!"

And they brought in hamburgers!

Beautiful hamburgers, the patties thick and juicy, steam rising in the cold evening air. The smell hit me first, that delectable aroma of grilled beef that speaks of backyard barbecues and summer evenings. Here we were, halfway across the world, our bodies aching from a day of hard riding, and someone had thought to give us this taste of home.

The hamburgers were a rare break from our usual fare: mutton. Breakfast, lunch, and dinner, mutton appeared in various forms. Sometimes wrapped in dough like dumplings that looked promising but weren't. Sometimes just...mutton. Living on the steppe, mutton wasn't just a meal choice; it was practical survival. Sheep were efficient converters of precious grazing land into protein. Understanding this didn't make it any more palatable to my western taste buds, which staged a silent protest at every meal. Julie taught me her survival trick early on: "Add ketchup!" It helped, but barely. The scarcity of familiar food made these hamburgers feel like a feast—each bite was a small celebration.

Now, I did not generally go crazy over hamburgers, but there is something incredibly comforting about familiar food when everything else was new and strange. It reminded me of Charlie's backyard BBQs, especially during our annual pumpkin-carving parties. He'd man the grill with the same focused attention he gave his woodworking, carefully arranging hot dogs and hamburgers like pieces of a puzzle. Kids would swarm around him, drawn by both the smell of food and his magnetic energy. He'd tease them mercilessly, doing his goofy dance while flipping burgers, making up ridiculous songs about proper hot dog–cooking techniques.

Those parties always expanded beyond pumpkin carving. Someone would inevitably bring a softball and bat, and suddenly we'd have an impromptu game going in the side yard. Later, as dusk settled, he'd hitch up the trailer for hayrides, packing it with straw bales and as many kids as could safely fit. He'd drive slow loops around the property, deliberately hitting every bump, the children's squeals of delight mixing with the autumn wind.

The familiar comfort of the hamburgers here in Mongolia hit differently, a reminder that while food could transport you home, it could also mark how far you'd come. I ate as much as I could, which wasn't much given my still-fragile stomach, but each bite felt like medicine for my homesick soul.

We covered 67K on Day Five for a total of 336K, or 209 miles.

9

Day Six

AKA, Not a Rest Day

Date: September 16, 2022
Distance: 67K, or 42 miles

The only thing that got me through Day Five was the thought that Day Six was going to be our rest day. For hours, I had clung to that promise like a life raft in rough seas. Carly and I had plans. Oh, did we have plans! There would be sleeping—glorious, uninterrupted sleeping. There would be bathing of some sort, maybe even washing our hair. There would be reading and picture-taking and a moment to remember that we were more than just lumps of pain riding endlessly across the steppe.

When Julie overheard us discussing our plans, her words hit like a bucket of cold water: "Tomorrow isn't a rest day. That will be the day after tomorrow."

Carly and I looked at each other in dismay. The hope drained from her face as quickly as it was draining from my heart. "Are you serious?"

She was.

How could this be? My tired brain tried to do the math, numbers slipping away like water through my fingers. We were supposed to ride for ten days. We had ridden for five already, right? And there was to be a rest day in the middle. But then confusion crept in about when our last riding day would be. If we rode for ten days, with one rest day, then shouldn't we be back in the city by Day Twelve? The dates weren't aligning with that logic, and it was becoming increasingly important to my psyche to know exactly when this was going to end.

"Help me understand!" I pleaded with Julie.

She explained that there were ten days of riding, but the first and last days were half-days, so they counted as one. My head hurt trying to process this new reality.

Haven, bless him, broke it down for me like he was explaining it to a child. In my exhausted state, I counted it out on my fingers.

Day One: half-day

Day Two: full day

Day Three: full day

Day Four: full day

Day Five: full day

Day Six: full day

Day Seven: rest!

Day Eight: full day

Day Nine: full day

Day Ten: full day

Day Eleven: full day

Day Twelve: half-day

Day Thirteen: back to civilization

In other words, today, Day Six, was not the rest day. I grimly went through my morning routine. Sadly, Tai Chi was not part of the morning. Instead, butchering was happening.

Butcher

There is something primal about being part of killing an animal and butchering it for your meal. Something life-affirming, as ironic as that seems. Something empowering about doing something hard and ugly for the goal of survival.

There is also a beauty in it. A kindness and gentleness. I imagined serial killers saying these very same words, and the thought made me shiver.

I wanted nothing to do with it. Not because I was squeamish—that wasn't it at all. It was because every time I saw a butchering, I was transported back to our garage with Charlie, to the many times we processed deer, bear, sometimes a goat or a cow. Charlie's method of execution wasn't graceful like our Mongolian guides'—he killed with a gun, not the quick, almost loving knife movement that had been described to me here. Their animal died quickly, without visible signs of stress. It was like watching a ceremony rather than a killing—or so I had been told.

The crew treated it as a celebration. For them, having an animal to butcher meant abundance, survival through the coming winter. I understood that celebration of abundance because Charlie had been the same way. A freezer full of meat made him feel rich, made him feel secure. It reduced his fear of a future of making do without. With a freezer full, he knew his family would be fed. He thought about things like that.

Wood in the woodshed, meat in the freezer, flour and sugar in the pantry next to canned goods. These were how Charlie measured success. Growing up poor had taught him the value of these things.

He would have loved it here.

I saw much of this same attitude in Mongolia. Riches measured in the things for survival. Having an animal to butcher was something to celebrate, not take for granted. We riders were invited to witness this. Carly and Haven accepted the invitation. Carly especially seemed to embrace it, a glee in her eyes that reminded me of my daughters during our family butchering days. They would gather in the kitchen, one cutting steaks, another wrapping, a third working the grinder for hamburger. They would sing songs and tell stories, making memories over sharp knives and butcher paper.

My role had always been gofer. I picked up pizza for hungry workers, ran to the store for tape and butcher paper. Otherwise, I stayed out of it. I got my fill of slicing meat after working in an Alaskan cannery the summer I turned twenty-one. My job was slime line, pulling salmon off the conveyor, quickly gutting them and sending them on to be processed. At the start of the season, I felt pretty badass operating that knife. By the end, I was just going through the motions.

So, I chose a few extra precious moments of sleep instead, letting the sounds of the crew's laughter and singing drift through my tent walls, a reminder that even in the midst of death, there is life. Even in the midst of loss, there is celebration.

Mud or Stars

"Two men looked out prison bars. One saw mud, the other saw stars."

I don't remember when I first heard that phrase—sometime in my youth—but it has lived in my mind ever since, surfacing now as I listened to the crew's joyful butchering celebration through my tent wall. It always struck me as profound, this idea that two people could experience the exact same circumstances so differently.

For me, it means you get to choose how you experience things. In this situation, two men were in the exact same circumstances, but their experience of it was vastly different. One had chosen to look out and see only the mud. Only the misery. Only all the things that were wrong. The other looked out and chose to see the stars. The beauty that existed in spite of all the misery.

I had always thought of myself as a stars person, able to see the fun and beauty in all things. But this last year, since Charlie passed away, I had been decidedly a mud person. Once you looked at the mud, it was hard to look away. There was just so much of it, and it sucked you in. In the year since Charlie passed, I became firmly entrenched. Every creak in the house became the absence of his footsteps. Every sunset became another day he didn't see. Every task became a reminder of what was missing.

This is not the best frame of mind to arrive and participate in an endurance event. Attitude is everything. I knew this. I knew that my attitude was contributing to my misery, and if I could just fix that, everything else would fall in line. I knew this. I *knew* this. And yet, I struggled.

But there was magic here. Sometimes the only way to get yourself focused on anything but the mud is to get in deep, so deep that you suddenly find yourself sick of it. Being here in Mongolia, I could feel myself wanting to look up. Wanting to see the stars. Wanting to see the good and the joy that still existed.

I was still not sure which I'd see when I emerged from my tent—the mud of another grueling day of riding ahead, or the stars of being part of something bigger than myself. Maybe both are true. Maybe that's the point.

Riding Day Six

I awoke on Day Six, full of hope. I thought, *sleep is a magical thing.* Plus, my sleeping bag was exceptional.

I want to talk about my sleeping bag for a moment. I want you to understand its importance. I know it is a tiny thing, but damn, it never let me down. When I crawled into my tent, it was a little oasis of things that I had complete control over. Choosing my sleeping bag had been a very deliberate decision. Above all, I wanted to be able to sleep at night, warm and comfortable. I couldn't imagine anything worse than trying to face the challenges of the day if I had been lying awake and cold all night.

That sleeping bag, and those moments alone in my oasis, were the reason I woke up every morning feeling hopeful and ready to try again. It was money well spent.

I went through my now-established routine: bathroom, granola, water bottles. Each motion had become its own kind of prayer—not the formal kind I grew up with, but the wordless kind that comes from learning to find sacred moments in simple tasks.

At breakfast, Brandon appeared with athletic tape covering his mouth. It was a strange look. "What is that for?" I asked.

"My lips are chapped. This will keep me from picking at them," he said.

I wondered what he thought was going to happen when he removed the tape, and then decided it wasn't my problem and vowed not to be around when he did it.

When it was time to mount up, I made my way over, picking out my horse by the saddle he was wearing. Today's pony was new to me. His coat was white patches blazing against a background of deep chestnut, like someone had splashed paint across his side. Not a uniform color, but a landscape of its own.

He stood apart from the other horses, head slightly turned. Not disinterested. Observing.

I approached slowly. Not a direct line, but an arc, the way you might approach a conversation with someone you're just getting to know. His ears flickered. Not pinned back in warning, not fully forward in excitement. Just...listening.

My hand moved first—not to touch, but to be seen. Palm open, a gesture of hello rather than ownership. He didn't move toward me, and he didn't move away. He just continued that steady observation.

Something in the set of his shoulders spoke of readiness. Not tension. Not submission. Possibility.

When I swung into the saddle, everything changed.

It wasn't just contact. It was recognition. His body shifted beneath me—not tensing, but awakening. Those ears that had been neutral now pricked forward, electric with curiosity.

"Hi!" he said to me. "Nice to meet you! Did you know we are on an adventure?"

"Oh, yeah!" I answered. "I had forgotten!"

And just like that, we were no longer two separate beings. We were a single story about to be written.

I called him "My Little Pony" after the Hasbro toys of my youth.

Julie said to me, "Oh, you are riding Lhaagva's personal horse. That is a high compliment. He wouldn't let just anyone ride him."

I felt deeply honored. And then Lhaagva rode up and adjusted my hands on the reins. I exchanged a look with Carly, who said, "He's saying, 'don't you ruin my horse!'" and we laughed.

He said some words to Julie, who interpreted, "That horse is much more skittish than the other horses. You need to stay on top of him. Don't let him bolt."

My Little Pony did not bolt on me. In fact, I may never again be on a horse so responsive. My Little Pony and I just felt in sync. I leaned forward, and he went faster. I sat back, and he slowed. I thought about moving to the left, and we moved to the left.

He asked, "Do you want to go faster?"

"Yes!" I said.

"OK! Let's do it!" and we raced to keep up with the big horses. And then we started passing them. It was easy. We only slowed when we threatened to pass Baagii.

Carly laughed and said, "I wish you could see him run! His little legs are moving twice as fast as the others."

The joy took the edge off the pain. For the first time in days, maybe longer, I was seeing stars instead of mud. Here I was, on a paint pony in Mongolia, actually having fun. The morning sun caught his white patches, making him glow against the endless green of the steppe. His enthusiasm was contagious; each eager stride seemed to say, "Isn't this amazing? Aren't we lucky to be here?"

Tom decided to ride a little way with us and was given Kevin Smith. I was anxious about this. I rode behind Tom, monitoring him. I wasn't sure what I thought my watching him would do. It turned out the answer was "nothing." There was nothing I could do.

Kevin Smith tripped, went down on his knees, Tom went flying over his head, did a somersault, came right back to his feet, and got right back on that horse.

Well, OK, then. I stopped watching Tom like a hawk.

About mid-morning, Julie called a halt and announced, "We have officially reached the halfway point."

My first thought was, *Halfway!*

My second thought was, *Only halfway??*

I decided to choose the first response.

I looked over at Carly. How long had it been since I'd done that? An hour? She was hunched over, not smiling. I tried to assess. Was there something new and concerning? Was she working through things like I was, and there wasn't anything anyone could do about it? To test the waters, I said, "I'm so encouraged! There is less in front of us than there is behind us!" She did not say a word. She just glared at me. "Too soon, huh?" I asked. And she just nodded.

I felt that. Legit. We had come so far to only be halfway.

Still, we rode on. I tried mind games like, *Every step is one less step I need to take.* And *At some point, this will all be a memory.* Instead of cheering me up, these thoughts depressed me, and my earlier joy faded. Here I was, back in the mud again, watching my euphoria from My Little Pony slip away like morning mist.

In dialectical behavior therapy, DBT, they talk about living in the moment. I studied DBT because two dear people in my life have the diagnosis of Borderline Personality Disorder. This is a debilitating disorder that can often lead to loss of employment, destroyed relationships, and homelessness. The suicide rate is very high with this diagnosis. The people in my life dealing with this diagnosis struggle to manage. Some days are better than others.

I wanted to understand them and support them the best I could, so I read about dialectical behavior therapy and found many things that I could apply to my life. Its primary goals are to teach people how to live in the moment, develop healthy ways to cope with stress, regulate emotions, and improve relationships with others.

Staying in the moment means not letting your mind race down

imaginary paths of what the future will be like. One way to do this is to name something happening right now for each one of your five senses.

This is great, unless the present moment is actually terrible. At this point in the ride, my five senses list was this:

Feeling: Every hoof beat reverberated through my knees and ankles. My spine felt like a stack of broken dishes. Even my fingertips ached from gripping the reins. I was having difficulty sitting up straight. OK, that's not helping. Moving on.

Smell: Covid dulled this sense, making it my weakest. But if I really focused…there it is. Horse sweat and leather, sun-warmed hide. It smelled like childhood summers and county fairs. Like comfort. Maybe this exercise wasn't completely useless.

Seeing: Mostly I was watching for gopher holes, my world narrowed to the few feet of earth ahead of my horse's hooves. But when I dared to lift my gaze—oh! The sky sprawled endless above us, clouds herding themselves across that perfect blue. Green-and-gold grasses rippled like waves. In the distance, mountains rose blue as smoke against the horizon like a promise. But just a quick look, because, you know, those gopher holes.

Taste: Dry thirsty mouth. Quick drink and then moving on.

Hearing: The wind. Always the wind. It doesn't just make noise; it owns the soundscape, turning everything else into whispers and echoes. A lonely song that seems to come from everywhere and nowhere at once.

I want to convey to you that this experience was not easy. I didn't come to do something easy. I came to do something epic. That didn't mean I also had to be happy about it. At least not in the moment.

And then it started raining.

We stopped, and we all got our rain gear out.

The Voice of the Wind

The wind howled across the steppe, its voice familiar as a childhood memory. I'd known this wind before, or one like it, back when I was four years old, standing in our yard in North Dakota, Twin Buttes Reservation, Mandan Indian Nation. My father and I stood together in a blizzard, the world gone white beyond our fence line. Our house sat unsheltered from the relentless wind, and the yard—huge in my memory—was a canvas for winter's art, summer's dry brown dirt transformed into drifting snow sculptures. I peered into the white darkness, trying to see my school. Beyond that was nothing.

I turned to look at my father for reassurance and accidentally faced into the wind.

The wind hit so hard I couldn't breathe. I stood there in silent panic, trying to figure it out.

Dad rescued me. He scooped me up, and I buried my face in his neck. The wind couldn't get to me there. I pulled in gulps of nice, warm air.

North Dakota winters could mean weeks at a time when it wasn't safe to go outside. My parents taught me to both love and fear the wind.

If a door suddenly opened, they would say, "Oh, Windy just arrived." And I would think we had invisible company. Company was rare and always exciting—even invisible company.

But there were also stories about getting caught in the wind. Stories of people, usually a woman, left alone on the prairie in a tiny house, with only the sound of the wind. It drove people crazy.

It was better if you forgot the wind. Ignored it. Focused on other things, like reading stories, mending farming equipment, sewing, cooking, anything.

If you didn't ignore it, if you listened to the wind too closely, you could hear voices. Voices of people outside, calling for help. They begged to be saved.

In the winter, when the wind stirred the snow into a visually solid white wall, farmers would run a rope between the barn and the house. This was so they could hold on to the rope and be assured that they would be able to follow it to their destination. In the winter, the daily chore of feeding the livestock was a risky venture. And more than one farmer never returned, only to be found in the spring thaw.

Wind was no joke in North Dakota.

Even if the sky was clear, the wind could kill you. The first rule of survival: When you go for a walk, always walk facing the wind. In this way, you won't walk beyond your ability to survive. If you walk with the wind at your back, you can be fooled into thinking it's a nice warm day and end up walking too far. Only to turn around and be frozen to the bone before you get home.

Like all forces of nature that demand respect, humans tried to tame the wind with stories and songs. One song was about the names of rain, fire, and the wind—Tess, Joe, and Maria respectively. It wasn't until years later that I discovered this was a pretty popular song. I didn't know that then. I thought it was just my family's song. I only heard it in our isolated home on the prairie, played by my mother on her guitar, while the wind sang back up. In my child's mind, I thought we might be the only people on the planet who hadn't been frozen or blown away. The wind made all the outside sound like folks were out there dying.

Our connection to the outside world was tenuous at best. When we had a signal, the radio played news and Paul Harvey, "The Rest of the Story." We didn't have a TV. I had been given a record player, and I played my records over and over. I had records with stories. *How the Grinch Stole Christmas* was one of them.

We were often without power. On those days, we sat around our gas cook stove with the oven door open to keep warm. When we were with power, we sat in the back bedroom, the warmest room in the house.

There, in our winter sanctuary, I was cozy with blankets. My dad cleaned his guns. My mom read to us. *Chronicles of Narnia, Wizard of Oz, The Return to Oz, Heidi*. The wind howling in the background made all these stories seem more real.

But our true refuge lay below. My parents hung a swing in the cellar. I think most kids don't actually spend a lot of time in their cellars, but in ND, this was one way we were able to include physical play when stuck inside for weeks on end. I swung on that swing and sang. I had my own little orchestra down there—a cricket sang along with me, and sometimes a frog would join us. A single light bulb on a string lit the space. It did not occur to me to be afraid. Here, in my underground playground, the wind was silent.

Day Six—Afternoon

Once I was in my rain gear, hood up, it was like I was in a cocoon. A warm, cozy, safe cocoon. And it was a relief, almost as nice as when I hid my face under my father's chin. There was a barrier between me and the wind. I hadn't realized how it had been wearing on me. With this little space, I was able to relax a little and actually look around.

The rain transformed our world into a monochrome painting of grays and silvers. Driving rain is rain that is propelled by the wind. It hits harder than normal rain and comes at you from the side or an angle, rather than from above. It stings any exposed skin like tiny needles. And in this weather, more things were blowing around—tumbleweeds and stray garbage, among others.

Out here on the steppe, maybe the most dangerous thing we were likely to come across was blowing garbage, just because these things would cause a horse to bolt.

So I held the reins the way Lhaagva taught me and rode forward in my little cocoon. I peeked out at the world from the shelter of my hood, and this was what I saw.

Rain falling in gray-blue sheets, hitting the ground sideways and bouncing back up, before falling again.

The sky above us had become a battleground. Roiling clouds, black with the promise of more to come. They moved like an invading army, their dark mass consuming the horizon.

My team became ghostly shadows in the gray curtain of rain, spreading out across the landscape. We had been in a tight group, following a dirt road under some power lines, but at some point, we turned left and headed across the bare expanse, and now the rain blurred the distant horizon. One by one, my companions faded into the murk until they became darker shapes against the gathering gloom. Baagii and Haven led the pack, as always. Carly and Brandon were behind me, and behind them were Julie and Lhaagva. But then we were spreading out, getting farther apart, and Brandon was veering off to the side.

Panic fluttered in my chest. I rode, looking forward, watching for flying objects that might scare my horse and keeping track of where we should be going while looking back, trying to make sure my entire team was accounted for. All the while, I was growing increasingly concerned for Brandon, who seemed to be only looking down and decidedly moving away from us.

Relief washed through me when Julie caught up with Brandon and they turned our way, followed by more relief when Carly passed me and I knew she was safe. Through it all, the rain fell and the wind howled, turning our world into a wild watercolor painting where nothing held still.

We rode and rode. The world narrowed to the rhythmic splash of hooves and the constant drum of rain against my hood. At some point, I started to notice unrest with our leaders. Julie rode forward to talk with Baagii and then back to speak with Lhaagva, and then over to talk with Tom and Bayaraa in the van. And then the van passed us and drove ahead. When Julie came by again, I asked her what was up, and she said the van went ahead to see if they could find camp.

We rode in the gathering darkness, no one really sure we were headed in the precise direction we needed to be going. The rain had stolen our landmarks, leaving us adrift in a featureless gray world. Then off on the horizon, far to the right, we saw headlights flashing at us. Like a beacon in the darkness, they beckoned us that direction and we plodded on.

Eventually, we entered a grove of saxaul trees. More like over-grown bushes, really, their gnarled branches reaching about twenty feet high. They grew thick in the sandy soil where no grass dared take root, creating a maze-like forest along the river valley. These were small trees, compared with what I was used to, but they were thick. They swayed in the wind and blocked our view. Once we were in the grove, it was a maze of twists and turns, and then we rounded a corner and there was our crew.

Let me repeat that. *And there was our crew.* Those words deserve their own moment of reverence. After endless miles of uncertainty, seeing them there was like spotting a lighthouse through a storm, that instant when exhaustion gives way to pure relief. If you've ever been lost, really lost, and then suddenly found your way home, you know the feeling. It's not just seeing what you've been looking for; it's the full-body realization that the searching is finally over.

The trucks were all there, and they were frantically trying to set up the ger in the middle of this storm. We rode in and dismounted and collapsed into chairs to watch the show.

The storm we'd been watching stalk us across the steppe finally pounced. They had the frame up already and were wrestling with the sides and roof, everyone's hands fighting the wind. Watching the crew work together—cursing, laughing, shouting directions over the gusts—brought me back to so many other mad dashes against weather: running out with my sister to cover the hay with tarps just before the rain hit, that chaotic scramble at summer camp to rescue laundry from the drying line.

I couldn't sit any longer, so I got up and offered to hold down a piece. Soon the whole team was stationed at different points, human anchors while they strapped it down. We formed a chain of bodies against the wind, each person bracing against the storm. Zulaa ran the strap around the outside and pretended to tie me down as well.

Wind played with us, lifting our hair and pulling on loose corners, but in the end, we had a shelter.

I found my chair again and fell into it. Haven had already collapsed into the chair next to me. He joked, "Did you see the ger *I* set up?"

"Yes, I did!"

We covered 67K on Day Six for a total of 403K, or 250 miles.

10

Day Seven

Rest Day

Date: September 17, 2022
Distance: 0

I had a dream the morning of rest day. I had purchased a giraffe, thinking I had purchased a camel. And I said, "This looks nothing like a camel!" I wasn't sure what specifically the dream was an analogy for. There were so many things that were not what I was expecting. But rest day, oh, sweet rest day, did not disappoint.

Our tents were near one another, and they all looked out over the water. We were each in our private spaces, but we could talk to one another. We slept. We lay out on the grass. We read. I took pictures. Brandon was up at dawn and attempted to walk to the nearest town that we could see in the distance. But after realizing it was almost 10K away, he jogged around the camp instead.

We set up one of those camp showers—a bag that you fill with water and hang up high and then stand below while you open a valve on a hose. The highest we could hang was from the door of the truck, so we had to squat down to get under it. Carly took the first one. I took the second. The water was warm. The air was cold. But in the end, I was clean, and that was wonderful.

Each horse was inspected, but not in the casual way I was used to back home. Baagii and Lhaagva caught them one by one, and I watched their methodical process with fascination. They set up IVs containing B vitamins and electrolytes for each horse, a practice I'd never seen before but accepted as part of endurance riding protocol. While the vitamins dripped, their hands moved over each horse with practiced precision, checking every inch of hide and muscle. They used stethoscopes to listen to both heart and gut sounds, their faces intent with concentration.

I'd seen them perform similar examinations during our evening stops and breaks, minus the IVs, which were reserved for rest day only. Their thorough attention to the horses' health reminded me that these weren't just our transportation; they were athletes performing an incredible feat of endurance. The IV bags hanging beside each horse were like athletes getting their post-marathon recovery supplements.

Haven and I set up chairs and read our books. Here is something funny. I told you about almost everything I packed for this trip. I told you about the weight and space restrictions. I told you that I agonized about what to keep, and what had to stay behind. I didn't tell you that somehow, I managed to pack four books. I left my helmet behind, but I brought four books. Is that ridiculous or what? But I didn't know how much down time I would have, or if I would be speeding through books and desperate for something to read. Apparently, boredom is a deep-seated fear. I brought two Chet and Bernie mysteries by Spencer Quinn and two books by David Lagercrantz, *The Girl in the Spider's Web*, and *The Girl who Takes an Eye for an Eye*.

Brandon ran by us, then came to sit with us with his book, then went running again. I wondered what medicinal concoction he was on that made it difficult for him to relax on a rest day.

Carly isolated and focused on self-care.

Some of the crew had the tire off a vehicle, doing some mechanical work. I watched in confusion. I was not a mechanic, and I didn't know what the issue was, but the solution appeared to be a block of wood wrapped in rubber (an old tire?), which they were attempting to pound into the space between the wheel and the body of the vehicle. They talked away in their soft musical language and laughed, and then tried again.

Watching the crew repair the truck with nothing but a block of wood and determination, I was struck by their easy collaboration. No cursing, no blame, just quiet conversation punctuated by laughter. Even when things went wrong, their good humor never wavered.

Charlie and I did not have that kind of working relationship when it came to projects. He'd approach projects with his buddies like a contact sport—every setback met with creative cursing, every solution celebrated with equal vigor. That's how they bonded, apparently: through shared frustration and collective problem-solving.

But with me, it was different. The first time we tried to build something together—a bookshelf to house my large collection—I misread everything. When he cursed at a stubborn screw, I heard anger directed at me. When he swore at a warped board, I took it personally. While his buddies would have sworn right back and dived into fixing the problem, I retreated into silence.

Charlie noticed. Of course he did. He started treating me with exaggerated care, explaining every step as if I were made of glass. "Now, honey, I'm going to measure this twice, because that's what good carpenters do..." The gentler he got, the more frustrated I became. We were terrible project partners.

Eventually, we worked out a system. Our fireplace mantel, for example. We wanted a TV there, but we didn't want to look at it. I designed a wooden box with a front cover that was attached using magnets, and Charlie built it. I painted a scene on the front with the quote "Not All Who Wander Are Lost." Above that were blocks of wood that Charlie cut, then I drew dragons on, and then he carved out. We learned to collaborate by respecting our differences rather than trying to force similarities.

Now, watching these Mongolians work, I wondered what Charlie would have thought of their approach. Even Tom—usually our resident cynic—commented on it. "Have you noticed," he said one evening, "how they never lose their shit? Even when everything's going wrong?"

I had noticed. It was so different from the workshop dynamics I knew—no cursing, no drama, just steady progress and shared laughter. Another kind of male bonding, another way of solving problems together. Charlie would have been fascinated by it; he might even have learned from it. I know I did.

I thought about my irritation on Day Three when we arrived to find our tents weren't set up. I had arrogantly assumed the crew's only job was to tear down tents, drive to the next place, and set up tents. What could be so hard about that? But watching them today, I realized how naive that assumption had been.

The logistics of moving a group of riders across 700 kilometers of wilderness were relentless and interlocking: meal planning and preparation; tent setup and breakdown; maintaining a sheltered eating area; caring for the horses through the night; and gathering and tacking them each morning. They managed all this while keeping up morale with their constant good humor. Forty-five miles by car might have been nothing, but doing it while orchestrating this complex operation was something else entirely.

When evening came, I found Haven, and we took a walk. We meandered across the sand and explored the riverbank. The conversation was uncomplicated. The day's rest had softened the hard edges of our exhaustion, leaving space for something gentler. Haven had on a clean white shirt, and I learned that he had brought two: one for the first half of the ride and one for the second. I marveled again at this bold choice.

The riverside camp stretched out around us, a landscape of quiet activity and soft conversations. Together we found Carly and Brandon, and we wandered through brushy grass, talking about our dogs, and broken engagements, children—the messy, beautiful fragments of lives we'd temporarily set aside during our ride.

For dinner, we were served Mongolian BBQ, but not the kind

you find in American strip malls. The air in the ger grew thick with the rich aroma of the lamb that had been butchered the previous day, now cooked with potatoes and carrots. Steam rose from the pot in fragrant clouds, carrying the mingled scents of meat, vegetables, and something earthier—the hot rocks they added to hold the heat.

When they pulled the rocks from the pot, the rocks glowed with captured warmth. We were each given one to toss between our hands. The smooth surface radiated heat into my palms while the cooking oils left a slick sheen on my skin. The oils from the cooking and the warmth from the rock were meant to be healing. We were told to put the rock on areas that were painful and it would help. I looked down at my aching body. I was going to need more rocks.

The ritual of the meal unfolded with both ceremony and casual fellowship. They poured everyone a shot of vodka, and toasts were made. The food was brought into the ger in two large bowls and set in the middle. We had two locals join us. With the gravity of a sacred rite, Baagii served us each a piece of meat, starting with the oldest to youngest. Julie, Haven, Thomas, me, Carly, Brandon, and then the guests. Only then were we released to grab what we wanted out of the bowls with our bare hands.

There was ceremony to the process and a free-for-all at the same time. It felt ancient and immediate at once, this sharing of food, this breaking of bread together in the middle of nowhere, continuing traditions that stretched back centuries.

After the meal, the crew and the visitors all left the ger to socialize among themselves, leaving just us four around the table. The space felt different with just us riders—more intimate, like a late-night dorm room conversation where secrets might spill out. Haven had been trying to remember a song for several days. He said it was a sort of monotonous song that would seem to fit well with his riding pace. Not a favorite, but one that he thought was kinda funny. In the warm glow of the ger's light, we had a little signal, and Carly used it to search for his song. It was "The Piano

Has Been Drinking." We listened to it and laughed and thought about the story of it. How all these things are going wrong and the guy singing it is blaming everything else and denying his own obvious part.

The music opened something in us. We decided to each share a song that we knew every word of. Not necessarily a favorite song. We had to tell the story about why we knew all the words, and then we found it on Spotify for the rest of us to listen to.

Carly went first. She sat forward in her chair, exhaustion momentarily forgotten. Her face was lit with joy as she laughed at her young teenage self who heard this song and thought, *This is what love is!* and she sang it from her teenage heart with gusto. The firelight caught the shine in her eyes, and I loved watching her face animate with her joy.

Caught up in the warmth of the moment, I wanted to give her some of that back, so I shared a song from my youth. My mom had one cassette tape of Johnny Horton that we played over and over on road trips. I knew them all by heart, but I chose to sing "Ol' Slew Foot" beginning to end, with all the sass and southern accent I could muster.

The gentle crackle of the fire filled the pause before Brandon's turn. He searched the phone to find his song and started to play it. I heard the first few notes and asked, "Oh, is this the song I think it is?"

Of course, no one knew the answer to that. But after a few more notes, the familiar melody twisted in my gut and I said, "It is! Ugh, I hate this song."

Brandon immediately turned it off. The silence fell heavy between us. I regretted my words immediately. My stupid self-centeredness barged its way into the spotlight, stealing Brandon's moment.

The song was "A Whiskey Lullaby." I have always hated that song.

Why do I hate that song so much? It is difficult for me to get words around it. The lyrics swim up to form a memory, whether I want them or not. The song is about a man who loved a woman, and when he was rejected, he started drinking until eventually he dies. The woman felt so guilty that she, too, drank herself to death.

I think it romanticizes a tragic situation in which someone uses an external substance to try to fix internal emotional pain. And while I know it is a complex situation, the anger rises in my throat like bile.

The warm intimacy of our circle suddenly felt too close as it became all mixed up in my head with an incident that occurred when I was about four years old. I was groped by a drunk man who wandered into our yard where I was making mud pies. The memory came in fragments: the gritty feeling of wet dirt on my hands, my dad arriving on the scene very shortly and shouting at me, "Rachael, get over here!"

Even now, decades later, I could still only remember Dad yelling at me a handful of times. As an adult, I realize he wasn't yelling at me at all. He just wanted me away from that man. But at four years old, I thought I had done something terrible.

The large hands running over my body, the smell of stale alcohol and days old sweat on unwashed skin—these things form the word "alcoholism" in my mind. And I reject the idea that a broken heart is justification for this behavior while at the same time acknowledging that this is an over-simplification.

Looking at Brandon's face in the firelight, I realized that moment, in the ger, out in Mongolia, was not about me and my feelings about a dumb song. It was Brandon's moment, and I stole it. I did not share this story with the team. Instead, I said, "I'm sorry. Tell us why this song is one song you know all the words to."

Brandon shifted in his chair, fingers tracing the rim of his cup. He shared about how prevalent alcoholism was in his family. How some of his best bonding moments with his father were drinking stories, and, at the same time, some of his worst moments with his father were also drinking stories. Brandon had a complicated relationship with alcohol. Even on this trip, Brandon was the first to purchase alcohol and enjoyed staying up late drinking with Tom and the support crew. At the same time, he said in the ger that night that he hates, truly *hates*, what alcohol did to his family.

The fire crackled, sending sparks up into the darkness. Outside, the wind whispered across the steppe. Inside, we sat with these complicated truths. Some love letters are written, it seems. And some are sung around campfires in languages the heart understands better than the mind.

Life doesn't come in nice, neat packages, does it?

11

Day Eight

Broken Stirrup

Date: September 18, 2022
Distance: 75K, or 47 miles

Rest day had worked its magic. I woke up feeling hopeful. I met Haven for Tai Chi, the sun painting the steppe gold behind us while Julie captured our silhouettes with her camera. One of those photos now hangs blown up on my wall, proof that I once did something really cool.

The morning promised possibility right up until I approached my horse. That's when I noticed the problem. My left stirrup was bent at an impossible angle, like it had been run over by a truck. I looked at Lhaagva in confusion and pointed at the stirrup. He made a face, and then he and Baagii pulled on it until it straightened out. They nodded at me, satisfied.

I wasn't.

But I mounted up anyway. What choice did I have?

Since we were on the second half of the ride, it was time to start taking our turns in the beautiful Mongolian saddle that would later be auctioned off at the Gala. We were each to ride 20K in the thing. Carly decided that this day, the day after rest day, would be her time to make it happen. Julie documented the event on video, and we all cheered as she mounted.

Two minutes into our ride, that damn stirrup was out of shape again.

Let me try to describe what this was like. When you are in the saddle, small adjustments, like the length of the stirrup, make a big difference in your long-term comfort. The same is true for everything you do. *Ergonomics* is the term that applies here. For any prolonged activity, the goal is a neutral position. Any awkward position will cause problems.

In the saddle, both feet go into stirrups, and they should fit so that both feet are supported equally, slightly turned out, heels closest to the horse. To understand what was happening with this broken stirrup, I invite you to stand up right now. Stand with your feet slightly wider than shoulder width. Now, take your left foot and turn it so that instead of standing on the bottom of your foot, you are standing on the outside of your foot. Now walk around like that.

Do you see how this is a problem?

I was OK for the first 5K, but then I was absolutely not OK.

Our pace continued at the trot. Each hoof beat was a hammer strike against my ankle. Every down beat, every single down beat, slammed my ankle. I tried riding with my feet out of the stirrups, but then the stirrups were flopping independently, and I worried about what my horse thought of all that extra action.

I tried to adapt. I rode with my feet in the stirrup but as if I were riding bareback, putting my weight in my thighs for the upbeat.

I thought I was doing OK, but at break, I had to put my full weight on that left side in order to dismount. Lightning shot through my leg, and I cried out.

The stirrup had taken the shape of an elongated, stretched-out rubber band. My hands shook as I showed it to Lhaagva. Again, he and Baagii took turns pounding on it and pulled on it until it was back in the normal shape. They smiled at me as if to say, "See! All fixed."

Bile rose in my throat. I was not impressed. How could they possibly think this was OK? But I was too tired. My whole body felt hollow with exhaustion. I went and sat with my team.

At lunch, we repeated this game. I had a limp now.

After lunch, I decided this wasn't going away. Pain had become my constant companion, so I might as well try to make friends with it. It was time to start figuring out distractions. I had two songs I wanted to sing, but I could not remember the words. One of them I could only remember a vague sense of living on the plains, and it would perplex me for weeks. Finally, long after I got home, I remembered it. It was *Home on the Range!* The irony of forgetting *Home on the Range* while riding across an actual range wasn't lost on me. How could I have forgotten those lyrics?

At least I knew the other song was by Elvis, so I told my team at break, and everyone started singing Elvis songs until finally someone landed on the one I was looking for. It was the song about what wise men have to say and how sometimes you *Can't Help Falling in Love.* The words felt so true in that moment. Like I was falling in love—you know, like that tiny little spark of joy that sits in your belly. But it wasn't for any specific person. It was for my whole team.

Carly Gets Engaged

The afternoon's misery was a raw ache that settled into my muscles like cold, damp clay. The relentless Mongolian Steppe stretched around us, a sea of ochre and dusty green rippling beneath an immense sky, when two motorcycles approached our group. The growl of their engines cut through the persistent whisper of wind-bent grass, and Baagii greeted them with a joy that seemed to lift the very air around him. He called a halt, an unusual interruption that sent a ripple of relief through our exhausted group. The sudden stillness was a balm, punctuated only by the soft snorting of our horses and the distant tinkling of a horse bell.

Shortly, a third man joined. He stood out like a peacock among sparrows, a walking canvas of color and texture. His deel shimmered with a life of its own, the silk pulling the afternoon light into it and throwing it back as deep blue, then purple, then blue again. Each movement sent new wavelengths of color rippling across the fabric, the embroidery catching the light like delicate frost. The traditional swooping sleeves moved with a liquid grace, embellished with intricate threads that told stories of wealth and tradition. His motorbike gleamed with the same meticulous care, chrome and paint so perfect it seemed to absorb and reflect the harsh Mongolian sunlight. His smile was broad and knowing, a performance of charm that seemed to say he was acutely aware of the picture he made.

I tried to dismount with some semblance of grace, but my body betrayed me. The leather of the saddle stuck to my sweat-dampened legs, and my muscles screamed in protest. My dismount was more of a controlled collapse, my boot catching awkwardly in the stirrup before I half-slid, half-tumbled to the ground. The dust rose in a small cloud around my feet, thickening the crust of dirt and grime already etched on my skin.

I made my way to the community blanket, a worn, faded thing that smelled of wool, horse, and countless miles of travel. I collapsed onto it, feeling the rough weave against my abraded skin. Each movement sent a new wave of muscle pain through my body, a testament to hours of hard riding.

Haven was already there, his usual grace abandoned for a controlled fall. The blanket seemed to absorb his weight with a soft whisper of fabric. Carly arrived next, her face a map of exhaustion, looking like she would gladly never move again. Brandon dropped down beside us, his perpetual energy finally ground to a halt. His face was a mask of misery, dust caking the lines of sweat and exertion.

Tom appeared with his medical kit, the leather worn smooth from countless journeys. He took in our sprawled forms with a look that was equal parts concern and mild disgust. "You lot look like shit," he announced.

We lay there in shared exhaustion, the wind of the endless steppe still vibrating through our bones. The sound was constant: a low, persistent hum that carried the scent of dry grass, distant livestock, and the faintest hint of wood smoke from some far-off ger. No one spoke. No one needed to. The simple act of being still together was comfort enough, our bodies a collective ache, our breathing synchronizing like a single, tired organism.

Meanwhile, on a blanket a short twenty feet away, a very different exchange was happening. Laughter and talk in the uniquely gentle Mongolian language felt like noise on a radio playing two rooms away until, suddenly, Julie barked out a laugh. Her laugh was sharp and unexpected, like a stone dropped into still water.

I turned, surprised. When had she joined our blanket? The movement sent a fresh lance of pain through my shoulders, muscles protesting every slight shift. We all looked at her, our collective gaze heavy with curiosity.

"They don't know I can speak Mongolian," she said, her voice rich with mischief. "They are talking about us!"

Like wounded animals suddenly alert, we all perked up, the exhaustion momentarily forgotten, replaced by the electric curiosity of being the subject of secret conversation. The air seemed to tighten with anticipation. "What are they saying?"

"Well, the older one asks if you guys are any good at riding."

Carly and I exchanged a look. Our bruised bodies answered that question better than words could. "What does Baagii say?" we demanded in unison.

"He says you're fine," she waved dismissively. "But now they are talking about 'foreign women.'" And then she laughed again. "That young man in the fancy deel, he is saying that it would be nice to marry a foreign wife, then you could travel."

The absurdity of it all. Here we were—broken, dirt-encrusted, every muscle screaming—being assessed as potential wives. The laughter bubbled up from deep in our chests, a release of tension that hurt even as it healed. Our bodies might have been broken, but our spirits were undefeated.

The young man in the silk deel—a walking piece of art—rose with a grace that seemed to mock our exhaustion. His silk sleeves caught the late-afternoon light, shifting from deep blue to rich purple with each movement. It was like watching a living painting move across the dusty landscape. He began wandering among our horses, each step deliberate, almost theatrical.

When he reached my horse, he noticed the broken stirrup. The leather was cracked, hanging uselessly, evidence of the day's brutal ride. He held it up, a smirk playing across his lips—part mockery, part genuine amusement. Even he knew it was ridiculous to be riding with such a thing.

Something protective flashed across Carly's face. She didn't like him criticizing my gear, a warrior's instinct, a sisterhood forged through shared hardship. "I'm gonna go inspect his bike," she announced. "Just like he's inspecting our horses." Her voice was casual, but there was an edge of challenge beneath the words.

She walked over to it and did a slow circle around it, mimicking his earlier swagger.

The young man's reaction was instantaneous. He dropped my stirrup and practically floated across the space between them. His movements were a dance, silk rippling, boots barely seeming to touch the ground. When he offered her a ride, the invitation hung in the air like a challenge and a promise.

Carly hesitated, her weight shifting from one dust-covered boot to another. The old men—weathered as the landscape itself, skin like tanned leather, eyes bright with perpetual amusement—gave their blessing. Baagii's nod carried the weight of cultural permission.

I was half-worried he wouldn't bring her back, but I also wanted to see what would happen.

Before they could leave, pictures were demanded. Cameras appeared as if by magic, small digital devices incongruously modern against the timeless backdrop of the steppe. The young man's smile was pure electricity—bright enough, as we joked, to light up all of Ulaanbaatar.

He drove a large, careful circle around us, Carly perched behind him. The motorcycle's engine created a low growl against the wind's constant whisper. Later, we would tease Carly about her Mongolian boyfriend, or maybe even a fiancé, whom we were sure would have their picture blown up and hanging on his ger wall within a week.

We covered 75K on Day Eight, for a total of 478K, or 297 miles.

12

Day Nine

Horses Missing

Date: September 19, 2022
Distance: 50K, or 31 miles

I crawled out of my tent on Day Nine and carefully stood up, test-ing each joint like a soldier checking for wounds. My ankle held my weight, and I was thrilled. During the last hour of the ride the previous evening, I made sure Julie knew about the stirrup situa-tion. She said, "Oh, we can switch out stirrups."

The words hit me like a slap. I could not tell you how angry that made me. If switching out stirrups was an option, why the hell wasn't that done first thing?

But I kept this to myself. The energy required to form words felt like too much. I wasn't the only one suffering, and shouting wasn't going to help matters.

On this morning, though, I vowed to refuse to get on until that stirrup was replaced.

What happened instead was that there weren't any horses.

The absence struck me as bewildering at first, like walking into your kitchen to find all the plates gone. Fences are rare in Mongolia, so traveling herdsmen will hobble their horses at night. A hobble is just a rope tying three of the horse's legs together loosely. This allows them to walk and to kick out if they need to defend themselves. But a faster pace is difficult, and so horses generally don't wander far.

So when we woke up and there weren't any horses, initially, we were not too concerned. Besides, it was someone's job to stay awake and check on the horses through the night. The crew's faces stayed carefully neutral when the person in charge of that admitted he had fallen asleep. But he stated he last checked on them at 3 a.m. and they were all there, so they couldn't have gone far.

The first ripple of real concern crossed Baagii's face after he drove a large circle around the camp. And then a larger circle.

We saw some horses on the far hill and put a scope on them. The crew huddled around the scope, their quiet murmurs in Mongolian carrying notes of doubt. They didn't think they were ours, but they were across the river, so it would be hard to get close enough to know for sure.

With nothing else to do but wait, I decided it was time for a sewing project. I had intended to be taking video with my GoPro and had brought a strap to attach the GoPro to the front of my helmet, but since I didn't have a helmet, I hadn't been able to do that. But now that I had some free time, I decided to sew a mount onto the front strap of my water backpack.

I thoroughly enjoyed this morning. The forced stillness felt almost like a gift. The river flowed peacefully by us while birds chirped happily. We had ridden over a pass the day before and dropped into its endless green valley. The sky was the real show-off, with its ever-changing colors and cloud patterns. In another context, this would have been paradise. I'd have felt like I was in a scene from the Old West, but the Old West of my home country was a baby compared to this ancient land.

While I sewed, Julie got out the drone and flew it far and wide, her face tense as she searched the screen for any sign of our missing herd.

Meanwhile, I asked Tom to wrap my ankles. They were both competing for which could hurt more.

By mid-morning, the pretense of calm began to crack. We started to suspect the horses had been stolen.

We teased Carly, saying that her Mongolian fiancé had a lot of horses. It would be the least he could do to let us borrow some for the rest of our ride. Our laughter held an edge of hysteria.

Finally, Baagii arrived with the horses. They had retraced our path from the day before and were back up in the mountain pass. The horses looked sheepish, as if they knew they'd caused trouble, their heads low and ears flicking nervously. And we still had a long way to go that day.

Grim-faced discussions followed about how this was impacting our plans. Julie came to us and said, "We still have to cover at least 50K today, and we are going to be at a fast pace. We won't make our planned camping site tonight, but Lhaagva's in-laws live on the route and we will go there instead."

I approached my horse and my heart sank. The stirrup had not been replaced. "Julie, what about my stirrup?"

Julie spoke to Baagii and pointed at my stirrup.

Baagii had been up since way before dawn, looking for the horses. Exhaustion and worry carved deep lines around his eyes as he worried about their welfare and how we were going to cover the distance that day. He couldn't give a fig for my stirrup situation. He glanced at it, said something, and got on his horse.

Julie turned to me. "He says they don't have any spare stirrups to fit your Western saddle."

The last thread of hope I'd been clinging to snapped. I was dismayed.

And then she added, "Zulaa will be going into town today. He will try to find something."

Barely Controlled

Empty promises. More waiting. More pain. What could I do?

I thought about control, how it feels when you're holding on to it by your fingernails. Charlie understood that kind of control. Not the easy kind that comes when everything's going right, but the harder kind that you choose when everything in you wants to explode.

Charlie's real strength lay in knowing when not to fight at all. I remember watching him handle a situation that could have exploded into violence.

The man at Charlie's driver's-side window was drunk, aggressive, and spoiling for a confrontation. But Charlie's voice remained steady, almost gentle. "Have you been drinking?" A denial. "I can smell the alcohol." Each word measured, chosen with careful precision. In the backseat, the girls held their breath.

Charlie could have stepped out of that car. He could have met threat with threat. Instead, he chose to be the kind of father who makes his children feel safe in an unsafe moment. He told jokes, kept his voice light, and turned a potential trauma into just another Sunday afternoon inconvenience.

It wasn't until later, when he reached for my hand, that I felt the tremors running through his fingers, the aftermath of adrenaline, of choices made and violence avoided. That trembling told me everything about the man I'd married: His strength wasn't in his fists, but in his willingness to shake rather than shatter the peace.

His trembling hands told the story about the cost of choices made and unmade. About choosing your battles. About the kind of strength that looks like weakness to those who don't know better.

Charlie lived with chronic pain after his accident, each day a negotiation between what his body demanded and what his spirit refused to surrender. I watched him learn to navigate this, to find that narrow space between endurance and wisdom. Some days that meant pushing through. Other days it meant admitting defeat, though he never used that word.

Now, as I considered this horse with its broken stirrup, I understood something new about those moments. About how control isn't just about holding back anger; it's about choosing which pain you'll accept and which you'll resist. About finding that line between necessary suffering and needless heroics.

I thought I'd learned those lessons watching Charlie, but maybe some things could only be truly understood from the inside, when you're the one trembling with the effort of holding yourself together, when you're the one choosing which kind of strength you need to have today.

The whole crew was on deck, helping us get moved out, with everyone's anxiety ramped up. We had the same amount of ground to cover, but a lot fewer hours in which to do it. We needed to be moving! Even the cook, whose job never involved the horses, was there. He held my horse and our eyes met. His intuitive gaze turned to concern. "You OK?" he asked.

I gave a wobbly hand response. His worried face darkened a little. I said, "I will be OK," the lie tasting bitter in my mouth, and then asked, "Are you OK?" I was concerned for this young man who showed so much concern for me. He didn't appear to understand the question. Or it made him uncomfortable. He changed the subject and patted my horse. "Good boy," he said, and on this we agreed.

We rode hard. We galloped or fast-trotted. We never walked. Each downbeat sent lightning bolts of pain from stirrup to ankle, like the pounding of a finishing hammer to the outside joint. Teeth-gritting wasn't cutting it anymore. My world narrowed to a tunnel of agony. I worried I was going to have permanent damage, and it pissed me off that they hadn't switched the stirrups yet. There comes a point when you have to use some of that wisdom your middle age has earned you.

I made it to 30K.

"I can't do this, Julie," I said. The words came out barely above a whisper, but they felt like surrender. And I didn't need to explain further. She was fully aware of the situation. I'd like to pretend that she was impressed I'd made it that far.

We stopped, pulled off my horse's saddle, and I got in the medical van.

It was the best possible decision, and I hated it. The moment the van door closed, I felt like I'd stepped out of the story—no longer a rider, just a witness. I hated being separated from my team.

But it also gave me a chance to see everything from a different perspective. Bayaraa drove, and Tom rode shotgun. They didn't talk. The silence in the van felt thick compared to the constant wind outside. We drove behind the riders most of the time, but then we would speed up, get in front of them. Tom would get the camera out and turned on, and when we were in position, Bayaraa would take the camera and shoot some photos.

These photos would tell a different story than how it felt from the saddle. These were dramatic photos, the kind that belong in adventure magazines. We were riding into the mountains now, with the steppe stretching out behind us and framed by the valley walls. The evening lighting gave the world a unique color blend of reds and blues, transforming ordinary riders into silhouettes of legend.

From this new vantage point in the van, I saw us as others might—not as individuals struggling with our private miseries, but as a team bonded by shared hardship. The expressions on their faces told a whole story I'd been too consumed by my own misery to see. Haven, usually so serene in his Tai Chi movements, sat rigid with exhaustion. Carly's jaw was set in a hard line, her usual quick smile replaced by fierce concentration. Brandon's endless energy had distilled into raw endurance.

They weren't just riders anymore; they were warriors riding hard and nonstop. I saw grim determination on each and every face. My heart swelled with pride even as it ached with the knowledge that I should have been out there with them.

When we reached camp, I could see from the outside the toll riding was taking on our group. The last 20K of the day had been the same hard push. Carly, Brandon, and Haven were too tired to speak. They moved like sleepwalkers, trudging wearily to their tents. I was tired, too, but I was two hours of rest up on them, a rest I hadn't wanted, a reprieve that now felt like betrayal.

The van had given me perspective, but it had taken something, too. In saving my body, I'd lost my place in the tribe. I stood there watching them, feeling like an outsider, a ghost at my own funeral.

Alone.

It was strange to think about in some ways. I almost would have preferred literal torture just so that I could have been included as part of the group. I often thought of myself as the weak link. The one who would be the first to call it quits. The one least capable of enduring. And in this, I made myself the outsider. I made that call all on my own. No one else gave any indication at all that they thought I didn't belong. I went to my tent, just like the rest of the team. But sitting in my oasis didn't help. This was a moment when I wanted to be close to them. When dinner was called, no one told me. It was a minor oversight, but it stung.

Dinner at the In-Laws

We had shown up unannounced at the ger camp of Lhaagva's sister's family. Despite the unexpected arrival of several exhausted foreigners plus crew, they welcomed us with sincere grins and generosity. We crowded into their warm ger and watched our cook make pizza (pizza!) on the cook stove. The familiar comfort food felt surreal in this setting as we watched him tossing the dough, adding toppings, and then putting it in a covered frying pan. The scent of baking bread filled the ger, triggering an unexpected memory of Charlie and his infamous garlic bread. He had his own special recipe, which mysteriously acquired extra garlic whenever the girls brought boyfriends home. He'd sit there at our kitchen table, barely concealing his grin behind his own piece of over-garlicked bread, playing the role of protective father with just enough humor to take the edge off. Now, halfway across the world, I found myself smiling at the memory even as I sat there, aching and hollow, watching this display of hospitality. I wanted to speak Mongolian to our hosts. Express the gratitude I felt for the open doors. Could they know how deep kindness cut? When you're at your lowest, simple generosity can break you open. I smiled with earnestness, trying to convey my gratitude with a vocabulary of facial expression, posture, and miming.

Every available space had a butt on it. Five on each of the three beds. Two or three on every chest. Every chair taken. The ger was not large. On this evening, it held all of the family that lived there, all of our crew, and all of my team. The families obviously knew each other, and there was so much joy in the surprise visit. Conversations swirled, Mongolian and English intertwined. It reminded me of every family get-together I had ever been to.

I watched Lhaagva's sister prepare Airag, which was fermented mare's milk. I had been hoping for a chance to try this on the trip, having heard that it was a uniquely Mongolian experience. The familiar ritual of hosting guests transcended our language barrier. In my grief-sharpened awareness, every detail felt significant—the way she tilted the ladle to pour, how others instinctively knew when to fetch more fuel for the fire, the unconscious choreography of a family moving in their shared space.

A year ago, I would have focused on the exotic details, mentally collecting stories to tell Charlie. Now, I found myself noticing different things—how they leaned against one another while they worked, the casual touch between husband and wife as they passed each other, the way everyone gravitated to the warmth at the center of the ger.

These weren't tourist observations. They were reminders of what I'd lost.

But something else was happening, too. As bowls of Airag were passed around, I felt a different kind of isolation starting to crack. Earlier that day, watching my team from the van had made me feel like a ghost at my own funeral—close enough to witness but unable to participate. Now, in this ger, surrounded by people whose language I couldn't speak, I was paradoxically feeling more connected than I had all day. These strangers were showing me that belonging didn't always require shared words or even shared experiences. Sometimes it was as simple as passing a bowl, sharing warmth, and existing in the same space.

Someone noticed me shivering and wordlessly wrapped an extra blanket around my shoulders. The weight of it felt like an embrace.

I brought the bowl of Airag to my lips and took a tentative taste. It was the flavor of sour cream, but its consistency was more like water—warm, and not unpleasant.

The question of the evening was, "Are you religious?" Tom and Brandon were atheist. I don't remember Haven's answer. Carly said she was spiritual, not religious.

The question caught me off guard. In this day and age, saying you're religious feels almost like admitting to being judgmental.

Neither religious nor spiritual quite defined me. I didn't "believe" in God. The word *belief* feels too flimsy, too uncertain. That phrase was too shallow. It allowed space for disbelief. To say, "I believe in God" sounded as ridiculous as saying, "I believe in water. I believe in wind." These things don't require belief. They just are. And I knew God like I knew breathing.

And I knew God was there, in that ger, in that moment of connection across language and culture, in that offering of shelter to strangers.

"I have a deep and personal relationship with God," I answered.

Haven and Carly nodded thoughtfully.

That night, the sheep and goat herds moved down and among the tents, and all night the dogs barked and howled to keep the wolves away. I slept, snuggled cozy in my sleeping bag. *Tomorrow has to be better*, I thought to myself.

If only I knew what "better" would mean.

We covered 50K on Day Nine, for a total of 528K, or 328 miles.

13
Day Ten

Unraveling

Date: September 20, 2022
Distance: 70K, or 44 miles

Day Ten dawned like all the others. My hands moved through what had become ritual—granola, water bottles, ankle wraps—each motion a little slower than the previous day, a little heavier. I caught myself pausing between tasks, staring into middle distance, having to consciously remember what came next in a routine that should have been automatic by now. The others moved around me, their voices carrying through the crisp morning air, but their words blurred together like background noise. I double-checked my water bottles, then checked them again, not quite trusting my memory anymore. When Tom came to wrap my ankles, I couldn't remember if I'd already asked him to or not.

Brandon stomped into the breakfast tent, dropping his water pack roughly onto the table. "Did you hear the dogs barking all night?" he asked.

Irritation flared, his self-pity too close a mirror to my own dark thoughts. "Yes," I said, automatically shifting into the role of problem-solver. "They were doing their jobs, keeping the wolves away."

Brandon perked up at that news. "Really?" Just like that, his story transformed from a sleepless night of annoyance into an epic tale of survival. I recognized the shift in his energy, knowing I'd just helped him reframe his suffering into adventure. If only I could do the same for myself. Later, his Facebook post would include a reference to a wolf attack, and I'd pretend not to remember how close his morning complaints had cut to my own private misery.

Tom moved slowly with the ankle wrapping this morning. "My toes are getting cold," I said, the words coming out with more sass than I intended them. It was a small complaint compared to everything else, but today even my usual stoicism felt threadbare.

Tom stopped wrapping to take the cigarette out of his mouth. He glared at me, smoke curling around his face. "Do you want this done fast, or do you want it done right?"

I wanted it done right. I swallowed any further complaints and tried to focus on eating my granola. Tom put the cigarette back in his mouth, muttering something under his breath that likely was profane. Then, without ceremony or comment, he covered my toes with his warm hand. The simple kindness of that gesture, so at odds with his gruff words, caught in my throat. Sometimes compassion speaks loudest through calloused hands.

After our dinner of pizza the night before, a party started between the crew and the families, the kind of spontaneous celebration that marks Mongolian hospitality. An animal had been hunted that day, and I watched, fascinated, as they prepared it in a way I'd never seen before. They worked with practiced efficiency, removing the head and all the guts through the neck hole, then cooking the animal from the inside by inserting red-hot rocks—the Khorkhog cooking method.

In another life, I would have stayed to witness it all, to learn these ancient methods. But my exhaustion had its own demands. I went to bed while the party was still gaining momentum, their voices and laughter blown away by the wind. Out there, where the emptiness of the steppe made human connection precious, turning in early was almost an insult. But my exhaustion didn't care about cultural norms or missed opportunities. Another thing that marked me as "outsider."

Carly and Brandon stayed up for it, tasting the meat before bed. Tom joined them, too, passing around bottles with the crew, cementing bonds through shared celebration. The next morning, their hangovers added a different flavor to our collective misery. Our departure dragged, the crew moving with the careful deliberation of those who had honored tradition perhaps a bit too enthusiastically.

In spite of their after-party misery, the crew completed their tasks, and eventually, they swung my saddle onto my horse for the day. When they stepped back, I saw the solution that they found for my stirrup problem. It looked odd, but also amazing—perfectly shaped metal, an elongated D lying on its back. They attached them to the saddle using frayed red twine, and they dangled there like wind chimes in a storm, swaying wildly with each movement, but I loved them. The only thing that gave me pause was that there was a cage designed to prevent the foot from sliding through. The problem was that only my toes fit in the stirrup. I thought, *This is probably how I'm supposed to be riding anyway*, and I was just so grateful for a new stirrup, I decided not to complain about the cage.

Our departure was delayed further as Lhaagva and all his family needed pictures to mark the impromptu visit, a universal ceremony performed by families across the globe.

Finally, we were on our way, heading straight up into the mountains. For the first time since starting this journey, I felt completely in my element. The rocky outcrops and steep drop-offs were familiar friends, reminiscent of my rides in the Cascades back home. Where others tensed at the technical terrain, I found myself relaxing into a rhythm I knew by heart. With gopher holes no longer a concern, my eyes were free to scan the hills for mountain sheep and goat, to appreciate the wild beauty of this vertical world.

We climbed higher and higher until the van could no longer follow, the lack of roads forcing it to meet us on the other side. The terrain demanded a slower trot, but I found myself naturally taking the lead, my body remembering mountain riding on its own terms—the subtle shifts of weight, the careful positioning on steep traverses. I noticed Haven and the others hanging back, their eyes fixed on the ground immediately in front of their horses.

"Haven, look to your right!" I called back. "I don't want you to miss this amazing view!" For once, I could be the one offering guidance instead of receiving it.

Julie had chosen our morning break spot well: the planned camping place from the night before. It was spectacular, offering wind shelter, a deep waterfall-carved crevasse, rock pillars, and wind-swept trees. The kind of place that reminded me why I'd come all this way.

We pressed on, up and over ridges, rounding corner after corner, each crest revealing yet another climb. Despite my comfort with the terrain, exhaustion still crept in. When I finally asked for a break, apologizing as I did so, both Haven and Carly quickly expressed their gratitude. Even familiar challenges take their toll.

The van and lunch crew waited for us beyond the next bend, sheltered by a large rock that blocked the wind. I still couldn't eat much of the prepared food. Granola came to my rescue.

After lunch, things got harder.

The Breaking Point

I should have asked about removing those stirrup cages. They were like medieval torture devices. It was like being forced to run a marathon in six-inch stilettos, each step sending shooting pain across the top of my foot.

But the physical pain was almost secondary to the deeper ache of disappointment. Each morning, I'd wake with a fragile hope— maybe today would be different, maybe today would be the day I found my strength. Instead, the universe seemed to have other plans, serving up fresh layers of agony like a cruel chef preparing an endless tasting menu of suffering.

Julie shared a quote from a previous rider that distilled the Gobi Gallop into a brutal truth: "It's like training for a marathon, running the marathon, then getting up the next morning and running it again, then getting up the next morning and running it again, and on, and on."

This wasn't just a physical endurance test; it was a metaphor for grief, for survival. Each morning was another battle, another inexorable step forward when every fiber of my being wanted to stop. Relentless. That word echoed in my mind like a heartbeat.

Pushing through another shortened afternoon break, I understood why they typically did this ride in June. The spring rides had the luxury of long days, which meant more and longer breaks, so vital to stamina. Now with both winter and dusk breathing down our necks, every minute of daylight was precious.

I invented a survival game, a mental trick to keep myself moving forward. I'd select a distant landmark and declare it my 1K marker. When we finally crawled to that point, I'd choose another arbitrary target, creating a series of imaginary finish lines that kept me pushing onward. Each small victory was a lifeline, a way to fragment the impossible into manageable pieces.

Julie and Brandon both had GPS trackers. I didn't like to bug them with the age-old question, "How much farther?" but when I did finally ask, I learned that Brandon had turned his off. "It's too discouraging," he said. Which made sense. Whenever the distance had been voluntarily given to me, the truth was always more crushing than my imagination could bear, the remaining distance twice what I expected. Always twice.

My 1K game served a dual purpose. Beyond maintaining forward momentum, it forced me to look up, to remember I was actually riding through Mongolia—not just enduring but experiencing. The scenery deserved witnesses, even if those witnesses were broken. So I looked. I memorized. I stored images like precious artifacts to be examined later, when my body wasn't screaming its current protest.

Physically, I was disintegrating. Ankle pain had become an old companion, but now knee pain joined the rebellion. A new, vicious sensation burned across the top of my foot, each step a sharp reminder of my limitations. Putting weight on my foot was like walking across hot coals.

When I hit 20K, hope flickered. Surely camp had to be near. But when we rounded the next corner, only another great valley greeted us, stretching endlessly before our exhausted horses. No sign of tents anywhere. We rode directly down its center, and the sun, merciless and indifferent, began its slow descent, casting long shadows that seemed to mock our progress.

The steep descent into the valley tested our already-fragile balance. When Carly's horse tripped, I didn't see it. I only heard her sharp intake of breath, a sound that cut through the monotonous rhythm of hoofbeats. In an instant, she was back in the saddle, her resilience a quick flash of defiance against the unforgiving terrain.

Something shifted in her after that moment. Where exhaustion had previously draped her shoulders, now a fierce energy sparked. She urged her horse forward, moving closer to the front of our ragged line, her posture straighter, her pace more determined. It was as if the fall had jolted something awake in her, a reminder that survival wasn't about avoiding every stumble, but about getting back up.

I, however, was falling behind. Baagii moved with machine-like precision. His cold indifferent back moved steadily away with Haven and Carly trailing him like dutiful soldiers. Their silhouettes grew smaller, more distant with each passing moment, until they were nearly swallowed by the gathering gloom.

Brandon was my lone companion when the dog erupted from a ger camp, all teeth and fury. Its bark was a jagged weapon. We'd learned about dogs on the steppe—a chase could send our horses into a panic of bucking and wild-eyed terror. So we slowed, our horses matching our cautious pace, and we shouted back, a desperate attempt to assert our presence, to ward off the threat.

I watched, waiting for Baagii to notice our delay. Surely he would slow. Surely someone would see we were no longer with the group. But Baagii continued, unbroken in his relentless forward motion. I searched behind us for Lhaagva's reassuring presence, for Julie's watchful eye. But they were gone.

Twilight dissolved into an absolute darkness that seemed to swallow everything. The Mongolian steppe, which had felt endless during daylight, now became a black void of absolute uncertainty. Racing to catch up was impossible—we could barely distinguish ground from sky.

Julie's warning echoed in my mind like a prophecy: "Don't get separated from the group. If you get too far, your horse is going to do one of two things: bolt or not move." I gripped the reins with a desperation that bordered on prayer, my knuckles white beneath the growing darkness.

Brandon's voice emerged from the shadows, a thin thread of companionship. "Can't see them anymore, can you?"

"No."

Our horses began to whinny—not the soft communication of the herd, but raw, primal sounds of pure terror. Their cries cut through the darkness like shards of glass, high-pitched and broken. These were not the sounds of animals, but of creatures sensing something fundamentally wrong.

I remembered Roan's lesson about emotional transmission: Horses feel what their riders feel. So I forced calm into my voice, into my body, into every fiber of my being.

"You got this. It's going to be OK." The words came automatically, comfort offered to my horse echoing the whispered prayers I'd been sending heavenward since night fell. In that moment, I realized how often God's comfort comes through us to others even when we feel desperately in need of it ourselves.

Brandon was somewhere behind me, and I was glad he couldn't see my face. Our conversation fragmented—disconnected phrases about moving forward, about keeping steady hands, about not letting panic take control. His presence was the only thing preventing complete surrender to terror.

Then, just when I thought I understood the rhythm of the terrain, it dropped away without warning, and we were riding steeply downhill. A moment later we were climbing up again. Then down. Then up. Each transition arriving as a fresh shock.

The horse's whinnies grew more frequent, more desperate. Soft nickering transformed into high-pitched screams that seemed to say, "We are lost! We are alone. Something is coming!"

I strained my ears, hoping our horse's cries would carry back to the group. Hoping someone would hear. Hoping we weren't truly alone in this unforgiving night.

Headlights erupted from the darkness—bobbing, wild, and unpredictable. For a moment, hope flared hot. The van arrived, a brief punctuation in our terror, only to become another source of despair.

"You've got two more K!" they shouted, their voices distant and indifferent. Then they were gone, racing off presumably to find Julie and Lhaagva. We were nothing more than an afterthought, a footnote in their urgent mission.

Two kilometers. But in which direction? We could be moving straight forward, or we could be moving in circles. I had no way to know. No two kilometers had ever felt so long.

Steep inclines rose and fell like the breathing of some massive, sleeping beast. Black shapes melted into blacker backgrounds. Trees lurked just beyond perception. Water sounds whooshed somewhere close but invisible. Massive boulders materialized without warning, silent sentinels that we navigated around with desperate precision.

My horse's fear—a tangible thing—pressed against my own, merging and feeding on itself. Every sense was stretched to breaking—listening, feeling, hoping.

And then, a faint glow. So distant it might have been a hallucination. Camp lights? Possibly. But why did they seem so maddeningly far away? Why did salvation always seem just beyond reach?

The camp lights became a cruel mirage, making navigation even more treacherous. I surrendered any hope of avoiding obstacles, praying our horses possessed some innate navigation skills that had abandoned me completely. A dirt track emerged, a twisted path of deep grooves carved by a heavy truck that had passed through when the ground was soft and then frozen solid.

Our horses stumbled with increasing frequency, each misstep sending jolts of pain and panic through our exhausted bodies, causing us to cuss under our breaths in between voicing encouragement.

"You got this. Shit. It's going to be OK. Damn. Almost there! Holy fuck!

I sounded unhinged.

When we finally approached the camp, Tuya appeared from the edge of the firelight. She held my horse steady, a moment of unexpected gentleness in our brutal journey. I remained mounted, paralyzed. My body had forgotten how to dismount like it had forgotten its own alphabet, each movement a foreign language, each muscle requiring translation before it would respond.

Tuya's eyes met mine; they were filled with a sympathy that threatened to crack my remaining composure. I wanted to be lifted, to be carried, to be relieved of this final, impossible task. But there were no shortcuts. I was my own rescue.

I leaned into the pain, forcing my legs, arms, and ankles through movements that felt like betrayal. A whimper escaped as my foot touched ground and my legs refused to hold my weight. I collapsed, landing hard, grateful for the earth's embrace. Tuya's steady hand kept My Little Pony from bolting.

Somehow, I found my feet. Brandon moved beside me, a silent companion through this final descent into camp.

At the campfire, we found Haven and Carly, relaxed and laughing, as if nothing extraordinary had just happened. The scene was surreal, a stark contrast to our terrifying journey. From their perspective, they'd ridden confidently with Baagii, blissfully unaware of our harrowing experience. They'd assumed we were safely with Julie and Lhaagva.

"Well, that sucked!" I said, my words a massive understatement. They laughed.

They had no idea. A hysterical, unreasonable anger rose inside me, white-hot and uncontrollable. Brandon, standing beside me, understood immediately.

"You guys ditched us!" he blurted out, the words sharp with betrayal. "We had to stop because of that dog, and we couldn't catch back up in the darkness."

"We thought you were with Julie and Lhaagva," they responded, their casual tone adding fuel to my mounting rage.

And then, suddenly, I was worried again. Wait. Where were Julie and Lhaagva?

We turned, scanning the darkness. Dim figures moved at the edge of camp. I was already bracing myself—ready to go back out there for her if I had to. And then Julie's laugh rang out. Carefree. Amused. Completely unbothered.

She didn't need rescuing. And apparently, she hadn't given a thought to rescuing me.

I walked away.

In the confines of my tent, I attempted rational self-talk. *This is nobody's fault*, I insisted silently. *You are safe. Everyone is safe.*

But the words rang hollow.

If hunger hadn't been a biological necessity, I would have remained in my tent, a fortress of solitude and fury.

At dinner, my teammates traded stories of physical misery—a grotesque catalog of chafing, boob pain, "can we talk about my groin for a moment," constipation, and diarrhea. Their casual banter might as well have been white noise. I sat stone-faced, eyes fixed on the fire.

One of Carly's observations cut through my fog. "This is all so strange," she mused. "In what other situation would we share this much TMI with people we just met?"

I remembered a story. "Actually, there was this one time when I was completely naked and..." And I just stopped. The effort required to speak was beyond my strength. All eyes were on me, waiting for the next words. But I couldn't do it. The story that I was about to tell was really funny, and I had zero funny in me. I couldn't even smile.

"Never mind," I muttered, returning my gaze to the fire.

Protests erupted around me, but I just shook my head. The conversation flowed on, leaving me behind.

I was on the resentment train, and apparently there was no getting off.

I missed Charlie deeply. What would he have said to me right then? What advice would he have given? I'll tell you exactly. My Charlie would not have said a thing. He would have held me. He knew all my tells. He would have held me, and at the precise point that I was ready, he would have said simply, "Tell me about it." And then, he would have listened.

We covered 70K on Day Ten, for a total of 598K, or 372 miles.

14

Day Eleven

Broken

Date: September 21, 2022
Distance: 70K, or 44 miles

> "The ride is tolling, on mind and body. Takes a lot of mental stamina… The horses were doing it tough. I was doing it tough. My muscles were doing it tough."
>
> —Gobi Galloper, 2017

My hands moved mechanically through the morning routine—unzipping the tent, pulling on layers, reaching for granola. Each movement disconnected as if someone else was puppeteering my body. I didn't reach for the granola with anticipation. I didn't look forward to the first bite. I simply ate because eating was something bodies did.

Tom wrapped my ankles, and I watched the process with the detached disinterest of someone observing a stranger. My gaze slid past him, past the landscape, past everything. When he finished, I didn't even offer a thank you. The concept of gratitude felt as distant as the horizon.

My voice, when I found it, was deadpan and practical. "Zulaa, can you remove the cage from my stirrup?" He did so with no joking, sensing, I suppose, the barely controlled anger just beneath my surface.

When he removed the cage, a moment of possibility flickered, so faintly it was almost not there at all. I thought, *Maybe this stirrup issue is fixed now?* But my internal voice was a swift executioner of any nascent optimism. *Who are you kidding?* it hissed. *There's always something else waiting to break you.*

I sank deeper into the abyss.

Brandon might have taken his turn on the Mongolian saddle, the one destined for auction, a future I could not imagine reaching. But I was too submerged in my own darkness to be certain of anything beyond this moment of pure misery.

This was a mental landscape where no light could penetrate. Logic had become a distant memory. Intellectually, I knew this was the second-to-last day, but my entire being was convinced that this ride was eternal. A cosmic joke with me as the punchline. This endless, painful journey was now my entire existence.

My inner monster's voices dripped with poison:

"They'll make us ride 40K without a break."

"We'll keep going forever."

"No one cares that you're hurting."

"You're invisible."

"You don't matter."

Carly rode beside me, equally trapped in her own private hell. I wanted to reach out, to offer something—comfort, solidarity, anything—but I was empty. And even if I could have offered something, she would have rejected it.

The temperature plummeted like we'd stepped through a door between seasons—summer to winter in the span of a sunset. I was layers incarnate: wool long johns, wool socks, boots, chaps, fleece, puffy jacket, a Buff around my neck, hat pulled low, hood up, gloves on. And still, it was not enough. My feet became the epicenter of this bitter assault.

And so, I silently fueled the darkness, the resentment growing inside me and coming out in tears running down my face, which no one saw or cared about.

"You don't matter."

"No one likes you."

"You are weak."

"You are weak."

"I am weak."

Gifts and Gratitude

In spite of my absolute belief that we were never going to stop again, we did. And when I asked my bitter question, "How far did we go?" and I was told a cheery "20K," I was genuinely surprised. Not 40, after all.

My team, all exhausted, flopped down on our shared blanket. All except Carly, who got into the truck to get out of the wind.

I slumped there, feeling worse than I ever had in my life. No one spoke. Everyone was quietly getting food or closing their eyes. I just stared blankly into the middle distance.

I needed help. I had been praying, but with little hope of an answer. A quiet internal voice (God?) said, *Say it out loud.*

Early on in the ride, I had told my team, without hesitation, about the physical problems I was having. I said, and I quote, "I can't poop and I feel like I have to pee all the time." It was ridiculous to be telling these relative strangers this. And yet it had been easy.

This was not easy. This was telling them something much more personal. This was admitting to a weakness that I feared revealed deep flaws in my character. It was sharing something that could make me unlikable. Unlovable. Unworthy of respect and unworthy of friendship. It was my deep, dark secret. I was not, at my core, who I pretended to be. I was not tough. I was weak. And I had no idea how I was going to stand up, let alone climb back into that saddle, and finish the day's ride, let alone the entire ride. I lay on the blanket, broken.

Say it out loud, that insistent voice advised.

I had been praying this entire trip. I professed a deep faith in God, but I didn't truly expect him to rescue me. Bad things happen. They just do. And sometimes there is an easy way out. A simple "answer to prayer." And sometimes "the only way out is through it."

What happens if I can't get through it? I didn't mean just this ride. I meant everything, all of it. What does giving up even look like?

I stared into a black abyss of nothingness. Is giving up better? Is it a solution?

Say it out loud. That voice, full of patience and love, insisted again.

It was like this. My monsters insisted earlier that it was too late to pray. I was already in the thick of it. I should have done my praying before. The fact that I was miserable was my own fault. And I deserved what I was getting.

But I prayed anyway.

The monsters spoke louder, saying, "What can God possibly do? He isn't going to miraculously heal you. This is it. You have to live with it." And I *believed* them.

And still I prayed anyway.

But God could do something, and he did do something. It wasn't a miracle of healing, or a sudden wash of strength. It was the subtle, quiet voice giving me the precise words I needed in that one moment in time. Deceptively simple. *Say it out loud.* Easily dismissed—"that isn't going to do a thing"—until eventually I listened.

And that's the lesson I needed to learn and continue to struggle with. Listen and don't dismiss that small voice of wisdom. Because when I did say it out loud, everything changed.

"I need a better attitude," I said.

"I have something for that," Brandon replied.

For half a beat I just looked at Brandon, and then I burst out laughing. Haven did, too. The timing of his statement was so incredibly funny. Belly laughing, knee slapping, all of it. And Julie said, "Wait, I missed it. What was so funny?" And so we reenacted it. It was just as funny the second time. Stupidly funny.

When we caught our breath, I became serious again and told them, "I am stuck." The emotion behind those words threatened to spill down my cheeks again. "I am riding in this beautiful country and the *only* thing I can think about is how miserable I am. And specifically how cold my toes are, how much my ankles hurt, how each jostle on the back of that horse feels like a knife. I keep trying to distract myself, but it isn't working. I don't know what to do."

And then each person on my team gave me something.

Brandon had already made me laugh, which was medicine so pure and deep it cut into my darkness.

Julie, ever practical, got me into my deel. I thought only my feet were cold, but once I was in my deel, I realized *every* part of me had been cold.

Tom rewrapped my ankles, which was good because I think they had gotten too tight that morning and the cut-off circulation was not doing me any favors. And then he said to me in his gruff way, "How cold does it get where you live?"

"It can get pretty cold," I said.

"Colder than this?"

"Yes," I admitted.

"So, you have been this cold before, right? You know it isn't going to fucking kill you."

He said this not in a dismissive-of-my-pain way, but as a way to give me a tool. A mantra for my mind. "You have been here before. You survived. Your past success proves that you can do this. It didn't fucking kill you then. It isn't going to now."

Haven's gift to me was a hand on my shoulder and quiet words to tell me that, now that my top half was warm, the heat would flow down to my toes. And as he said it, a literal warm glow infused my heart.

I had not been rejected. I had not been dismissed. They got it. They understood. They cared.

When the break was over and we got back on the horses, I felt genuine hope. I was warmer, and I was channeling heat to my feet, wiggling my toes continually.

I had a bad fifteen minutes very soon after this, when my feet, which had gone solidly asleep, started to get circulation back. You know that pain when a limb has lost circulation so thoroughly? Like being stabbed with thousands of tiny needles, each one burning cold and hot at once. It radiates in waves, starting at your extremities and pulsing inward with an intensity that makes you catch your breath. It's your nerves screaming awake, each one firing randomly and desperately as blood returns. Your limb feels alien and heavy, like it belongs to someone else, yet every excruciating sensation reminds you it's yours. The agony builds to a crescendo before slowly, torturously subsiding into pins and needles, leaving you with the bizarre certainty that this relief is almost worse than the initial pain.

And when it hit, my first thought was, *I knew the good feelings weren't going to last.* But my second thought was, *Stop it. You know exactly what is happening here. You know this is temporary. It isn't going to fucking kill you.*

And, of course, it didn't. And the rest of the day, believe it or not, I had fun. Actual fun. Lunch was in the shelter of a shed. Carly and I were teased into eating more than we wanted to eat (though less than they wanted us to eat). Then Haven asked about shopping, and we made plans (we made actual plans like people who believe they have a future do) to go shopping Friday afternoon, after we checked into our hotel and had a long, hot shower.

During the afternoon ride, when we got to about 18K or so, I proactively asked for a break. I knew it was short of 20K, but I was no longer invisible, and I didn't want to let go of my good attitude. I knew that if I could just walk a few minutes, I would be able to handle the next stretch much better.

Our break was in a small grove of trees, out of the wind. It was peaceful. The sun warmed my upturned face, while friendship warmed my heart.

We remounted, and I was eager for the next leg.

Then we saw the rain.

Dark, boiling clouds that had been far away now turned their attention to us. They seemed to say, "Ahh, there you are, you tiny things. And now, we shall play." And with relentless determination, they bore down on our small group with all the glee of a playground bully about to get someone's lunch money.

We rode!

The cloud wall, with sheets of rain, hit the far hills, washing out the tracks we'd made much earlier that day. The sky in front was blue, and the setting sun was blinding. The wind was at our backs, both assisting the storm's progress and supporting our forward momentum.

It was a race! A race I feared we would lose because I had insisted that we take a break. We were going to get caught, and it would be my fault.

Our path led up a steep mountain, and while I could see the top maybe a half-mile away, I knew from experience that it wouldn't be the actual top, that we would crest it, only to discover another "top" at an equally far distance. And, though I had no real idea where we would be camping that night, I imagined that once we found the actual "top" of this mountain, we would then need to race down the other side until we found a valley and eventually our camp site.

There was nothing to do but ride into the blinding sun, trying to outpace the growling darkness behind us.

Even with sunglasses on, I could not look up for long, so I kept my eyes down, scanning the trail for obstacles. It was rocky ground here. The gopher holes were a thing of lower elevations, but that didn't mean the earth didn't have new surprises, and so I kept a vigilant lookout.

Then a shadow fell on my path. I looked up and realized the sun was being temporarily blocked by a stand of trees. The crest was still a good way off, but there was something much closer of interest.

I didn't immediately understand what I was seeing. Mounds of bright color? A truck? And then I said, "Are those *our* tents?" and Julie laughed. "Yes!" she said.

She had known all along we were very close to camp, but she let us take that break anyway, to give them more time to get tents set up. It was good timing because as we dismounted, it started snowing.

That night, around the dinner table, we teased Brandon about riding in the storm. He had spent the last of the ride at the front of the pack, and we told him that we had all been caught in a blizzard. We told stories of poor visibility and ice forming on our lashes and of snowflake trauma. He was really surprised. "I must have just been barely in front of it that whole time," he said, which was true, but that had been true for us all.

Finally, I put my hands to my face and said, "I can't do this anymore, guys!" I turned to Brandon. "There was no storm, at least, not until after we arrived."

We were up late that night, even me! It was cozy in the makeshift ger (the storm had come on too quickly for the full ger to be set up) with our wood stove. We laughed and told stories. We knew that this was our last night like this. I still didn't really believe it.

Watching the crew move around our campfire, each person naturally falling into their role—Tuya preparing food, Zulaa making everyone laugh, Baagii quietly ensuring everything ran smoothly—I thought about Charlie. Of course I did. How, as a single mom, everything had been extra difficult. Then he came along, and suddenly the hard parts weren't so hard anymore. Not because he took over everything, but because we each gravitated to what came naturally. He'd handle what I thought of as the heavy lifting—the yard chores, dishes, and laundry—and I focused on the things he felt were difficult, like helping with homework, paying the bills, and planning.

Now, watching our Mongolian crew work with that same unspoken choreography, I recognized something familiar.

Community isn't built by one person doing everything perfectly. It's built in the spaces between people's strengths, in the natural way they fill one another's gaps.

When I finally called it and left the ger, I couldn't find my tent. All the tents were covered in snow and looked like igloos. Once inside, I snuggled into my sleeping bag and thought, *This sleeping bag is the best investment I have ever made.*

We covered 70K on Day Eleven for a total of 668K, or 415 miles.

15

Day Twelve

North Dakota Blizzard

Date: September 22, 2022
Distance: 50K, or 31 miles

I awoke feeling hopeful. Still, I didn't really believe that this was going to be the last day of riding. I packed my things, same as every day. I hit the walls of my tent to knock off the snow. The morning became much brighter. I peeked out and saw six inches of snow. Time to break out the ski pants and goggles, I decided.

I stood up and immediately dove back into my tent for my camera. The morning was spectacular—the not-quite-risen sun made the far hills glow. White, misty clouds drifted above like soft apologies for last night's rowdy behavior.

The conversation this morning was easy, and I listened with half an ear while trying to capture this perfect sunrise on my camera. First there was the recognition, that moment when the mountain caught my eye. Then a series of micro-adjustments: three steps left, crouch down, tilt slightly. Each movement a hypothesis tested with a click of the shutter. I played with angles, searching for the one that told the story I saw in my mind. The sun shifted behind a cloud—I waited. Click. There. That's the one. But maybe...one more, just to be sure.

And while this was going on, the comfortable conversation continued. Haven chuckled, sharing a story from the night before—apparently Tom had tried to crawl into bed with him, unzipping Haven's tent and starting to enter before Haven drawled, "Tom, I'm that kind of girl." Tom had quickly realized his mistake, an easy one to make with all the tents looking identical under their blanket of snow. The story sent ripples of laughter through our morning circle, our breath visible in the cold air, mixing with the steam of our coffee and rising to join the morning mountain mist.

The crew started taking down our tents before we had fully vacated them, so I finished my morning prep in the ger. The final step was deels. We were all in them, even Haven, who only yesterday finally relented and wore a coat. It took the whole team to get us packed in our deels, and we felt like blue Michelin Men, or marshmallow monsters, when they were done. We took a group photo before we mounted.

It was my turn to ride the Mongolian saddle. My Little Pony stood ready. I climbed on, tucked in my deel, flipped down my goggles, tugged on my gloves, and felt very much like Han Solo riding a Tauntaun.

The wind blew the snow North Dakota–style. I was thankful for my tinted goggles. I loved my deel. I was so proud of My Little Pony, and riding in the Mongolian saddle was not terrible.

The crew was anxious to get moving. They worried the big trucks wouldn't have enough traction to make it up the mountain. It was tense, but entertaining, to watch them power up the hill. We cheered when they made it! Well, I cheered. Maybe the others did as well, but who knows? We were back on our isolated islands.

As we rode down the mountain into warmer elevations, layers of clothing started to disappear. My goggles went into my luggage at the break. After I did my 20 in the Mongolian saddle, we swapped it out for my western. Haven had the honor of riding the Mongolian saddle across the finish line.

My mind wandered, skipping around unimportant thoughts,

not really thinking at all when suddenly Julie called a halt. She grinned and shouted, "The GPS just clicked 700-K!"

"What?" and "How strange" were my initial responses. Five strides ago, I was on this epic journey across Mongolia, and now, suddenly, it was over?

It wasn't quite over, actually. We still had to get to base camp. We still had that final 20K to go. Our route was planned to be at least 700K, and they got it pretty close. But, still, we did what we set out to do. We got out the blankets and rested. Julie served champagne in plastic flutes. We toasted one another, and then we hauled our sorry butts back into the saddles.

Riding that last distance, surrounded by my team, I felt the weight of that number: 700 kilometers. Seven hundred. Back home, when people asked how far I planned to ride, their eyes would glaze until I said, "Imagine getting on a horse in Seattle and riding east on I-90. You'd be almost to Missoula, Montana, before you reached 700K." Then their eyes would widen with understanding.

Now we had done it, each kilometer earned through sweat, tears, and stubborn determination. Through broken stirrups and dark rides. Through moments of doubt so deep I'd thought they'd swallow me whole.

Accomplished. The word felt foreign. How many things had I thought impossible in the past year? Surviving without Charlie. Getting on a horse again. Riding across Mongolia. Each mile had been a negotiation with my broken heart.

The snow crunched under my horse's hooves as we prepared to continue. We still had ground to cover before the official finish line, but something had shifted. That number—700—rang in my head like a bell, like a promise kept, like proof that survival was possible. Not just possible, but worth the journey.

We stopped again at a summer camp for kids, currently deserted in this winter landscape. Julie said, "We only have about 2K to go, but we wanted to show you the summer camp, which, in addition to the school, is funded by your efforts. We also wanted to give you one more opportunity to just be with your team. When we ride over that hill, we will be greeted by camera crews."

I still didn't quite believe this was the end. It seemed like I should say something profound, but nothing came to mind.

We redressed in our deels for the cameras, had a last photo, and then headed out on the last leg of our journey.

We covered 50K on Day Twelve, for a total of 718K, or 450 miles.

A Hero's Return

We crested the final hill together, our horses moving in perfect parallel like a scene from an epic film. Baagii had warned us to keep tight control; our horses sensed home and victory. My Little Pony danced beneath me, eager to fly across the finish line, but I held him steady, unwilling to break this final formation.

The drones found us first, mechanical eyes buzzing around our heads like metallic insects, their whirr an alien intrusion after weeks of nothing but wind and hoofbeats. We were being watched, documented, and transformed from survivors into performers. The invisible lines that connected us—forged through shared exhaustion, terror, triumph—suddenly felt more real than the ground beneath our horses' hooves. Of all the people on earth, only these few beside me knew what this moment truly meant. This was my team!

Julie: Fierce catalyst of change, international nomad, and visionary with laser-focused determination. A Canadian who has made Mongolia her home for twelve years, building a school in the city's garbage dump neighborhood and creating the Gobi Gallop to support refugee children of climate change. She is the kind of woman who makes you want to be braver, to matter more, and to see the world not just as it is, but as it could be.

Brandon: Playful maverick, exuberant risk-taker, naïve innovator. A CEO who founded a company and lectures at universities, who decided to tackle the world's longest charity ride, and only then decided he better learn to ride a horse. Picture a Teletubby-esque figure with a GoPro helmet, sporting athletic tape on his lips to combat chafing, who considers a grueling jog a "rest day" activity. He is the kind of person who approaches impossible challenges with the enthusiasm of a child and the strategic mind of a global entrepreneur, solving problems with equal parts audacity and charm. Not because he has something to prove, but because the adventure itself is the point.

Haven: Introspective sage, hilarious Zen master, kindness personified. A Tai Chi instructor who waves at goats, laughs when wild horses run beside us, and listens with such depth that you feel truly heard. Picture a man so embarrassed by the meaning of his first name (Kenneth: "Handsome") that he'd rather talk about anything else. He moves through the world with a quiet presence that feels like both an anchor and a meditation, the kind of person who can turn a horseback journey into a philosophical exploration, who finds humor in the wildest moments, and who makes you feel safe without ever trying to.

Carly: Master of unspoken language, guardian of inner worlds, smile architect. A woman whose entire emotional universe can be read through the subtlest shift of an eyebrow—one raised in a "what is happening here?" moment of sharp awareness, another lifting in a half-smile that says, "Yep, that just happened." Behind her restraint lies a depth of experience so profound that silence becomes her most eloquent speech. She communicates volumes without a word, her face an intricate map of unexpressed stories, her smile capable of illuminating an entire landscape.

I am in love with each of them. Smitten to my core. They will forever be stars in my story. And I was so proud to ride through that finish line with these amazing people.

We were greeted by speeches, children playing traditional music on a morin khuur, and small hands offering food. Reporters with TV cameras focused on Julie while the rest of us stood attempting to look stoic and tough, while in reality we just looked dirty and tired.

Watching the children perform, I recognized something universal—that nervous energy of young musicians at their recital, the mix of pride and anxiety of a performance. The morin khuur's sounds, once so foreign, now resonated with the reason why we had ridden across Mongolia: to create opportunities for children who might otherwise be left behind.

A bee stung me—of course it did—as I stood trying to show genuine appreciation for the moment. We were ushered into a ger where a feast awaited, our dusty deels coming off to reveal that my shirt was inside out. I was a glorious mess of smiles, laughter, and tears, a survivor coming in from the wilderness.

This moment felt like stepping through a gate. Behind me lay 700 kilometers of raw adventure, of survival stripped to its essence. Ahead, the now slightly unfamiliar world of hot showers, clean clothing, and social graces.

We ate. We toasted. And somewhere beneath the celebration, I knew this transformation wasn't over.

I Can Do This

Someone asked me why in the world I would choose to ride the Gobi Gallop. It seemed to them a rather extreme action to take. My answer was a series of questions. What is it that drives humans to explore, to discover, to dream, to leave their comfortable homes in search of something more? Is it truly extreme to seek transformation? To deliberately place yourself in a situation that will challenge every preconception, every limitation you've placed on yourself? Throughout history, humans have undertaken extraordinary journeys—not because they were practical, but because something inside them demanded movement, demanded growth. Humans have been doing crazy things since the dawn of time. It seems odder to me that anyone who had the option would choose *not* to go.

After the feast, we were shown two gers, side by side: one for Carly and me, one for Haven and Brandon. The canvas walls of the ger hung heavy with years of accumulated dust and memories, the air thick with the lingering scent of our journey. Carly decided the next thing to do was to find the shower. We were to spend one night here before heading back to the city.

After Carly finished her shower, I went to take mine. When I got back to our ger, I found her shivering violently in her bed and moaning. I piled more blankets on her, stoked the fire, and went to look for Tom. I grabbed a couple sugary drinks for her while I was at it.

She was trembling not just from cold, but from the accumulated weight of our journey—weeks of physical strain, emotional turbulence, and suppressed survival instincts finally finding release. Carly was pissed to be getting so much attention, but I didn't care, and neither did Tom. Her body was finally reacting to the ongoing stress we had been through, and her emotions broke as well. Tom sat by her and talked her back from the emotional ledge. His rough voice, usually sharp with sarcasm, now carried an unexpected tenderness. Slowly, her shivering passed. I kept the fire stoked, the lights off, and let her sleep. It was hot in our ger, but I was OK with that.

When she woke up, we bundled up and took a walk to the river. The crisp evening air carried hints of sage and distant wood smoke. Julie joined us, and we sipped wine and talked about relationships and dogs and motherhood and loss.

Soon a couple ladies appeared and offered to bring dinner to the girls' ger. We would be hosting, it seemed, so we did a quick pickup of bras and clutter. Haven and Brandon came in. Lhaagva came by for a visit. He was feeling very fond of us all. He kissed each one of us on the top of our head and said words none of us could understand.

Julie and her husband joined us. It was comfortable, like hanging out with family was comfortable. We laughed and shared stories. I didn't want them to leave.

Night fell like a velvet curtain, thick and sudden, and we made our way to the bonfire that had been set for us. The flames pulsed like a collective heartbeat, drawing us closer with its warmth. We sat in a circle, each person illuminated equally, shadows blending behind us. Faces flickered between light and shadow, our edges softening like the logs slowly surrendering to flame. We shared this moment of collective breathing—of witnessing.

Lhaagva stepped forward. His beautiful tenor voice lifted in a song. Steady in rhythmic rises and falls. The Mongolian words sounded like a mystery. Tuya and Sarhaa's voices joined in blended harmony. Baagii, whom I'd seen as nothing more than a cold taskmaster, sang with a passion that startled me. His eyes caught the firelight—not looking at us, but somewhere beyond. Into memory, perhaps.

When they finished, silence hung like smoke.

"I want to sing something back to them," Brandon said. We looked at one another.

"Wise men say," Julie started, and I smiled, remembering that moment on the open steppe. Exhausted and trying to remember the words to "that one Elvis song" and the group of them singing every single Elvis song they could think of until we landed on the right one.

We all joined in with gusto and between us we remembered all the words, if not the precise tune. The fire crackled. Sparks spiraled upward, becoming indistinguishable from the stars.

Lhaagva and the crew drifted away first, their silhouettes melting into the darkness like a song fading. Julie and her husband followed, their goodnights soft, almost hesitant. And then—silence.

Just us four.

We had crossed continents. Survived impossible days. Shared pain that words could never fully explain. The space between us was filled with everything we hadn't said. The days of exhaustion. The moments of terror. The unexpected laughter. The private battles each of us had fought to be here, to survive, and to keep moving forward.

I looked at each of them and saw the journey etched in their faces. I was among warriors.

I was one of them.

Facebook Post: September 23, 2022

I want to bring you all up to speed on events, but I'm struggling to find words that are both concise for this format and yet comprehensive of the experience. The last two weeks have been raw in a way I've never experienced before. There are so many ways I could tell this story.

I could, for example, focus on the Mongolian cultural aspects. Share with you about how living on the steppe reminds me of what it must have been like for early pioneers in the US when your neighbors weren't just neighbors, they were part of your survival. And I could talk about the times we were welcomed into gers on cold evenings and what real authentic Mongolian BBQ looks like. Or the time a couple ran into their ger when they saw us coming, and ran back out with cheese and cream for us. And how we sometimes got an unexpected break when a herder arrived for a quick hello and a bit of news from our guides.

I could also focus on the horses. These amazing powerhouses carried us across impossible landscapes. My little paint, whom I nicknamed My Little Pony, became my closest companion. Together, we shared two simple goals: keep up and stay upright.

I could share with you the things that were overwhelmingly difficult and how my team came to my rescue over and over again.

A kind word, a timely joke, some off-color advice, and practical assistance as well.

I could talk about the weather. How at one point it was so hot I was riding in a sports bra, and at the end I had so many layers on that a bathroom break was more than a daunting prospect. But at least I was peeing again, so progress!

However I tell it, I should remind you that the whole purpose for this is to raise money for kids! This is something that came to the forefront yesterday. We rode through the finish line and were greeted like heroes. It was surreal. Cameras and drones, all buzzing away. And it was at this point I realized my shirt was on backward. Of course it was! I got dressed that morning in a snowstorm. And we had ridden 40K since then.

For the past two weeks, I have been living an alternate existence. Forced simplicity. Get up, get dressed, eat, ride, stumble back to my tent, and repeat the next day. Today I had a coffee in a restaurant, and at this exact moment I am lying on a comfortable bed in a corner hotel room looking out over the city.

Tomorrow we have the Gala! A night celebrating our journey. The Gala is sold out. There will be entertainment, auctions, speeches, and thanks. And my team and I will endure as we have all along.

Next week, when I am home, I will be cuddling up with my laptop, trying to process it all. I just might write a book.

16

How Does It End?

Last Day with My Team

The return journey to Ulaanbaatar was a photographic negative of our initial journey—the same landscape, but with all its values inverted, its shadows now light, its meaning fundamentally altered. Where we had once ridden forward with anticipation and uncertainty, we now retreated in solemn reverence.

Carly was wedged into the back, buried beneath a mountain of luggage. Her body, slumped and exhausted, was itself a topographical map of our journey: bruised hills, wind-carved valleys, rivers of sweat and determination.

At the hotel, we checked into our rooms and made good on the promise of a hot shower. It turned out to be everything and nothing. Water pounded away layers of dust, sweat, and memory, but some residue of the journey clung to me deeper than skin. My room felt alien—sterile, with a weird smell that wasn't quite home, wasn't quite the steppe. Loneliness crept in, a familiar companion I thought I'd left behind on the ride.

I called my family, desperate for connection. Their faces flickered on the screen, beloved and unchanged, and yet profoundly altered through the lens of my recent journey.

I didn't want to tell them about my journey, other than I

was safe. Instead, I hungered for news of their lives. How were the dogs? What did they have for dinner? What did they do while I was gone? These small details felt like a lifeline, grounding me after weeks of extraordinary experience. They were another gate.

Haven, Carly, Brandon, and I had made plans (was that just a couple days ago?) to go shopping on Friday, but Carly remained cocooned in her misery, her room a fortress against the world, politely declining our efforts to engage her. She just wanted to sleep, so we let her.

Meanwhile, Haven, Brandon, and I were determined to squeeze some adventure out of our last day, hiring a driver who navigated Ulaanbaatar's chaotic streets with wild abandon, making me just close my eyes and hope for the best.

We each had a mission. Haven sought a belt to accessorize the custom deel he'd commissioned from the seamstresses who had crafted our original garments—black silk that shimmered like a midnight Mongolian sky. Brandon was on a quest for the perfect gala suit, a victory outfit to commemorate our ride. I hunted for a Mongolian bow, a symbol of the mounted archery that had captured my imagination, and a wool shirt that might hold the memory of endless grasslands.

We found a belt, but the shirt and bow remained elusive.

Brandon's suit hunt led us into a world that felt like a fever dream. His internet research brought us to a tall building where official signage gave way to cryptic instructions directing us to descend into the basement. The entrance was something out of a noir film, a dimly lit hallway lined with mysterious doors, each one a potential portal to another reality.

The first door revealed a woman meticulously counting money, her fingers moving with the precision of an accountant. We closed that door, the soft rustle of currency lingering behind us.

Farther down the hall, Brandon found the door that led to a room of fabric—a textile tableau that seemed promising. Haven wandered further, discovering a room with a couch and a couple watching TV, their surprise at his appearance as complete as our surprise at finding ourselves in this labyrinth.

This leg of the suit hunt ended in defeat, and we retreated to the hotel's attached mall, a strange hybrid of international commerce and local charm. While Haven and Brandon wandered, I discovered a nail salon and made an appointment using my translation app. I would attend the Gala with a manicure!

That evening, we coaxed Carly from her hermitage for dinner. Haven, with a mischievous glint that had become familiar, produced a gift. "This thing I stole for you today," he announced.

A Christmas ornament. Such a small thing, yet loaded with meaning. Earlier, Carly had shared how she collects an ornament from every trip—a portable memory, a way of preserving the journey's essence. Knowing she'd been too ill to shop, Haven had thoughtfully bridged that gap, ensuring her tradition continued.

The next morning, we abandoned vehicular travel for our "black market" expedition. "Black market" was the term Julie used to describe it, though it wasn't illegal goods being sold, but rather a huge street market where thousands of vendors offered everything from traditional deels to modern electronics, all at negotiable prices.

Walking was faster than Ulaanbaatar's notorious traffic. I acquired a second suitcase, specifically to transport my deel. A wool shirt joined my purchases, along with hairspray so that I could do something with my hair, even though I lacked all other tools.

We split up then, to begin our transformation for the Gala. Brandon still didn't have a suit, but he had one more place to look.

In my room, nails freshly painted, I shed my riding gear and pulled on the gala dress. Its navy blue was striking against my tanned skin—its silver edging a match for the silver strands in my hair.

We met in the lobby so that we could all enter the Gala together. Haven looked as handsome as his first name implied. He said I had a wonder-woman vibe, and I was finally sure I picked the right dress. Carly arrived in a gorgeous black dress with a plunging neckline. Brandon didn't show. We decided to go up without him. Turned out, he was already there.

I felt very out of place at this fancy Gala, like a wild creature awkwardly dressed in civilian clothing. It was just so incredibly different from the rawness of the past two weeks. The people here were way above my financial station—businessmen and international ambassadors. I would have liked to speak to these people, but I found myself feeling inadequate. The polished floors and crystal chandeliers were an alternate universe from the wind-scoured landscapes, and my hands, still callused from reins and survival, felt awkward holding a champagne glass.

Between Carly still feeling ill, and my feeling timid, it was up to Haven and Brandon to work the room. Brandon embraced this, and he buzzed around, meeting people and telling stories. I was proud of him. Proud to be a part of his team. Proud of his ability to transform from campfire conversations about deepest fears to chitchat with the ambassador from China on one side and the ambassador from France on the other. But I kept close to Haven, who was a rock in this storm.

After a time, Haven, Carly, and I escaped to a quiet corner, where we tried to get our heads around the fact that what we did was huge. Tom found us, and we got to meet his wife, Claire, and she told us how she and Tom met. It was through a "no-strings-attached dating site." They got together for a wild weekend of sex and decided to just keep doing that. Eventually, they got married so they could keep doing it more conveniently. And I kinda love that story.

Brandon found us, and he was so disappointed. "There you are! I'm working that whole room by myself. And Julie wants us! They need pictures!" I knew he must have felt ditched once again. "I'm sorry," I said to him. "I will try to do better."

We went back, got pictures, and then we found our seats. We cheered for the many amazingly talented entertainers and considered dancing to the tunes of "Big Occ."

They showed a video of us on the big screen that Ashley had compiled and set to dramatic music. I wanted to watch it on replay, over and over. My team, larger than life, and so precious on that screen.

And then we were called to the stage, where we were presented with engraved trophies. Mine now sits on my mantel. Brandon's was confiscated at the airport for some reason.

Then there was the auction. We sat, the four of us, in all that noise. It was too loud to hear each other. We were, again, solitary islands. And it struck me that this was never just our story. This gala was never about us. In fact, the ride wasn't about us. We were just pieces of a puzzle that when put together revealed, it was always only about helping the children that were waiting back in that school by the garbage dump. It was the futures we might help create with each conversation, each connection made in this glittering room. What an incredible honor it was to be a part of that. I could have done better in that room, connecting to people. But I could have done a lot worse, by never coming.

Last Day in Mongolia

I spent my last day in Mongolia just like I spent my first day: with Julie. It was like a trip sandwich.

We were surprised to find that Ulaanbaatar had shut down the streets for the day. No cars allowed. Families were invited to walk the streets. It was a festival. Music and dance performances in the square. Families playing ball, roller skating and biking down the center of the street. People just milling around and smiling.

Julie and I talked about the disparities between the neighborhoods—what was happening here and now compared to what was available to the children of the ger districts. It was this disparity that Julie was fighting to fix.

I watched her joy as she watched the children perform in different costumes. She told me what she knew about the costumes, each one representing a different tribe in Mongolia. They honored their heritage in costume and dance.

When we parted, Julie hugged me and said, "I know you were hurting out there. I know how hard that ride was for you. But you handled yourself with grace. You can do tough shit!"

I walked away from that hug to the four-count beat of, "You are worthy."

The journey home passed in a blur of taxis, security lines, long flights, and shuttles until finally I found myself sitting at the bus station in my hometown, luggage piled around me as evidence of my trip. I felt the warm afternoon sun on my face and marveled at how familiar and foreign everything looked. I felt like an alien—on the outside looking in at my life. Familiar city, familiar traffic sounds, but I viewed it all through eyes that had witnessed endless steppes and star-filled nights. A woman hurried past, focused on her phone, and I wanted to grab her arm and say, "Did you know there are places where you can ride for days and never meet a fence?"

My daughter would arrive soon to pick me up, and I wondered if she would see the changes in me. How do you explain to someone that you left as one person and returned as another? That you crossed Mongolia on horseback, yes, but more importantly, you crossed the wilderness of grief and found yourself on the other side?

I knew then that I would write a book—not just to share the adventure, but to understand it, to map the territory between loss and healing, between who I was and who I had become.

When I walked into my house, the first thing I saw was Charlie smiling at me from his picture on my mantel. I stopped there and smiled back at him. "It's going to be OK," I said to him, and for the first time since his passing, I believed it. Then I started to unpack.

This is a love letter, dear one, written in the margins of grief and hope.

It is messy and imperfect, just like life. Just like love.

It is addressed to my Charlie. To my team: Haven, Brandon, Julie, Carly, and Tom. To my family and friends who hold me close. To my God who never let go. And, most profoundly, to myself. I am learning that love doesn't end. It transforms.

You—all of you—are precious beyond measure. You are the reason this broken world still shines with possibility. In the highest peaks and the darkest valleys, you are who I want beside me.

I love you.

Review Invitation

If *Mongolian Love Letters* moved you, made you laugh, or reminded you that the hard road is sometimes the right one, I'd be so grateful if you'd leave a review.

Reviews help independent authors more than I can say—they help readers find books that might matter to them, and they help this book find the people it was written for.

You can leave a review on Amazon, Goodreads, or wherever you purchased this book. Even a few sentences makes a difference.

Thank you for riding along.

Want to keep going? The journey doesn't have to end here.

Visit **rachaellundin.com** to see photos and videos from the Gobi Gallop—the horses, the steppe, the team, and the endless sky.

Acknowledgments

This book exists because of a village—and I am so grateful for every person in it.

To my editors, Tiffany Avery and Jenny Malnick: you made this book better in ways I didn't know it needed. Thank you for your sharp eyes and your care with my story.

To Daniel Pyle, for turning a manuscript into a book, and to Andy Bridge, for a cover that makes me proud every time I look at it.

To my beta readers—Kaylee Thompson, Nicole Warren, Codiann Lundin, Rebecca Sweeney, Helen Shaul, Danielle Worley, Kenneth Lipman, Jill Rodig, Chance Harris, Sandee Harris, Patti Bosket, Brandon Hutcheson, Kenneth Sumner, Tom Allen, Rachel Deskins, and Spring Miklosh—thank you for reading early, reading honestly, and telling me to keep going. Your encouragement was fuel.

To Julie Veloo, for building something extraordinary in Mongolia and for letting me be part of it. To the school and the children it serves—you are the reason the ride matters. To Haven, Brandon, Carly, and Tom: you are permanently written into my story, and I wouldn't have it any other way. To Baagii, Lhaagva, Tuya, Zulaa, and the whole crew who kept us fed, sheltered, and moving—thank you for your patience with a group of foreigners who had no idea what they were getting into.

To my daughters, my family, and my friends who held me up during the hardest year of my life: I see you. I love you.

And to Charlie—you already know.